Prepare for the Great Tribulation and the Era of Peace

Volume XLII:
January 1, 2006 – March 31, 2006

by John Leary

Queenship

PUBLISHING COMPANY
P.O. Box 220 • Goleta, CA 93116
(800) 647-9882 • (805) 692-0043 • Fax: (805) 967-5133
www.queenship.org

Dedication

To the Most Holy Trinity

God

The Father, Son and Holy Spirit

The Source of

All

Life, Love and Wisdom

Cover art by Josyp Terelya

Library of Congress Number # 95-73237

Published by:
   Queenship Publishing
   P.O. Box 220
   Goleta, CA 93116
   (800) 647-9882 • (805) 692-0043 • Fax: (805) 967-5133
   www.queenship.org

Printed in the United States of America

ISBN: 1-57918-299-2

Acknowledgments

It is in a spirit of deep gratitude that I would like to acknowledge first the Holy Trinity: Father, (Jesus), and the Holy Spirit; the Blessed Virgin Mary and the many saints and angels who have made this book possible.

My wife, Carol, has been an invaluable partner. Her complete support of faith and prayers has allowed us to work as a team. This was especially true in the many hours of indexing and proofing of the manuscript. All of our family have been a source of care and support.

I am greatly indebted to Josyp Terelya for his very gracious offer to provide the art work for this publication. He has spent three months of work and prayer to provide us with a selection of many original pictures. He wanted very much to enhance the visions and messages with these beautiful and provocative works. You will experience some of them throughout these volumes.

A very special thank you goes to my spiritual director, Fr. Leo J. Klem, C.S.B. No matter what hour I called him, he was always there with his confident wisdom, guidance and discernment. His love, humility, deep faith and trust are a true inspiration.

Equal gratitude also goes to our new spiritual advisor, Father Donald McCarthy, C.S.B.

My appreciation also goes to Father John V. Rosse, my good pastor who is retiring from Holy Name of Jesus Church. He has been open, loving and supportive from the very beginning.

There are many friends and relatives whose interest, love and prayerful support have been a real gift from God. Our own Wednesday, Monday and First Saturday prayer groups deserve a special thank you for their loyalty and faithfulness.

Finally, I would like to thank Bob and Claire Schaefer of Queenship Publishing for providing the opportunity to bring this message of preparation, love and warnings to you, the people of God.

John Leary, Jr.

Declaration

The decree of the Congregation for the Propagation of the Faith, A.A.S.58, 1186 (approved by Pope Paul VI on October 14, 1966), states that the Nihil Obstat and Imprimatur are no longer required on publications that deal with private revelations, provided they contain nothing contrary to faith and morals.

The author wishes to manifest unconditional submission to the final and official judgement of the Magisterium of the Church.

His Holiness, Pope Urban VII states:

In cases which concern private revelations, it is better to believe than to not believe, for if you believe, and it is proven true, you will be happy that you have believed, because our Holy Mother asked it. If you believe, and it should be proven false, you will receive all blessings as if it had been true, because you believed it to be true." (Pope Urban III, 1623-44)

The Catechism of the Catholic Church states:

Pg. 23, #67: Throughout the ages, there have been so-called 'private revelations,' some of which have been recognized by the authority of the Church. They do not belong, however, to the deposit of faith. It is not their role to improve or complete Christ's definitive Revelation, but to help live more fully by it in a certain period of history. Guided by the Magisterium of the Church, the sensus fidelium knows how to discern and welcome in these revelations whatever constitutes an authentic call of Christ or His saints to the Church."

Publisher's Foreword

John has, with some exceptions, reported receiving messages twice a day since they began in July, 1993. The first of the day usually takes place during morning Mass, immediately after he receives the Eucharist. If the name of the church is not mentioned, it is a local Rochester, NY church. When out of town, the church name is included in the text. The second occurs in the evening, either at Perpetual Adoration or at the prayer group that is held at Holy Name of Jesus Church.

Various names appear in the text. Most of the time, the names appear only once or twice. Their identity is not important to the message and their reason for being in the text is evident. First names have been used, when requested by the individual.

We are grateful to Josyp Terelya for the cover art, as well as for the art throughout the book. Josyp is a well-known visionary and also the author of *Witness* and most recently *In the Kingdom of the Spirit*.

Early in 1999 John's bishop established a special commission to read John's published works and to talk to him about his religious experiences. The commission rendered its report in June. By letter of June 25, 1999 John was advised to have an explanatory note printed in the front of each book. This note appears on page xi of this edition.

Presently, the messages are being reviewed by Rev. Donald McCarthy, C.S.B., John's spiritual advisor.

This first edition under these rules has resulted in a delay of 90 days.

Late in October, 1999 John Leary and Carol were called to the office of the Diocese of Rochester for a meeting with the Vicar General. The result of the meeting was that they (the Diocese) are now allowing John to publish under their obedience. John was cautioned against mentioning the subjects called to John's attention in the bishop's original declaration (see page xi). John was further ordered to have his spiritual advisor read and approve each book. This is being done on each book.

This volume covers messages from January 1, 2006 through March 31, 2006. The volumes have been coming out quarterly due to the urgency of the messages.

Volume I: July, 1993 through June, 1994.
Volume II: July, 1994 through June, 1995.
Volume III: July, 1995 through July 10, 1996.
Volume IV: July 11, 1996 through September 30, 1996.
Volume V: October 1, 1996 through December 31, 1996.
Volume VI: January 1, 1997 through March 31, 1997.
Volume VII: April 1, 1997 through June 30, 1997.
Volume VIII: July 1, 1997 through September 30, 1997.
Volume IX: October 1, 1997 through December 31, 1997.
Volume X: January 1, 1998 through March 31, 1998.
Volume XI: April 1, 1998 through June 30, 1998.
Volume XII: July 1, 1998 through September 30, 1998.
Volume XIII: October 1, 1998 through December 31, 1998.
Volume XIV: January 1, 1999 through March 31, 1999.
Volume XV: April 1, 1999 through June 13, 1999.
Volume XVI: July 1, 1999 through September 30, 1999.
Volume XVII: October 1, 1999 through December 31, 1999.
Volume XVIII: January 1, 2000 through March 31, 2000.
Volume XIX: April 1, 2000 through June 30, 2000.
Volume XX: July 1, 2000 through September 30, 2000.
Volume XXI: October 1, 2000 through December 31, 2000.
Volume XXII: January 1, 2001 through March 31, 2001
Volume XXIII April 1, 2001 through June 30, 2001
Volume XXIV July 1, 2001 through Sept 30, 2001
Volume XXV October 1, 2001 through December 31, 2001
Volume XXVI January, 2002 through March 31, 2002
Volume XXVII April 1, 2002 through June 30, 2002
Volume XXVIII July 1, 2002 through September 30, 2002
Volume XXIX October 1, 2002 through December 31, 2002
Volume XXX January 1, 2003 through March 31, 2003
Volume XXXI April 1, 2003 through June 30, 2003.
Volume XXXII July 1, 2003 through September 30, 2003
Volume XXXIII October 1, 2003 through December 31, 2003
Volume XXXIV January 1, 2004 through March 31, 2004
Volume XXXV April 1, 2004 through June 30, 2004.
Volume XXXVI July 1, 2004 through September 30, 2004
Volume XXXVII October 1, 2004 through December 31, 2004
Volume XXXVIII January 1, 2005 through March 31, 2005
Volume XXXIX April 1, 2005 through June 30, 2005.
Volume XXXX July 1, 2005 through September 30, 2005
Volume XLI October 1, 2005 through December 31, 2005
Volume XLII January 1, 2006 through March 31, 2006

The Publisher

Readers Please Note:

Bishop Matthew H. Clark, Bishop of Rochester, has accepted the unanimous judgment of a special mixed Commission set up to study the writings of John Leary. After reading the volumes and meeting with Mr. Leary, they testified that they found him psychologically sound and spiritually serious. They concluded that his locutions are not a fraud perpetrated on the Catholic community. Nevertheless, in their judgment, his locutions are of human origin, the normal workings of the mind in the process of mental prayer.

Of grave concern to the Bishop and the Commission, however, are the errors that have found their way into his writings, two of which are most serious. The first is called by the Church millenarianism." This erroneous teaching, contained in the first 6 volumes of *Prepare for the Great Tribulation and the Era of Peace,* holds that Christ will return to reign on the earth for a thousand years at the end of time. As the *Catechism of the Catholic Church* expresses it:

> The Antichrist's deception already begins to take shape in the world every time the claim is made to realize within history that messianic hope which can only be realized beyond history through the eschatological judgment. The Church has rejected even modified forms of this falsification of the kingdom to come under the name millenarianism ..." (CCC #676).

The second error is anti-papalism." While the Church holds that the Pope by reason of his office as Vicar of Christ, namely, as pastor of the entire Church, has full, supreme and universal power over the whole Church" (Vatican II, Constitution on the Church, #22), Mr. Leary's locutions select Pope John Paul II to be obeyed but his successor to be ignored as an imposter pope." This erroneous teaching is found in all the volumes.

Because Mr. Leary has reaffirmed the teaching and discipline of the Church and acknowledged the teaching authority of John Paul II and Bishop Matthew H. Clark and their successors, Bishop Clark has permitted these volumes to be published with this warning to its readers appended.

Visions and Messages
of John Leary:

Sunday, January 1, 2006: (Solemnity of Mary)

At Holy Name after Communion I could see Mary in front of Jesus and there was a brilliant white Light that shone down on Jesus and the angels were singing. Jesus said: *"My people, today's reading speaks of the shepherds coming to see Me in My infancy as they were directed by the angels. A Light came down upon the shepherds and a great multitude of angels sang to them.* (Luke 2:14, 'Glory to God in the highest, and on earth peace among men of good will.') *This great Light in the vision on My Blessed Mother and I was another intervention of the angels singing as the shepherds saw Me as an infant. It is My Light of grace that leads all of you to see Me even as you receive Me in Holy Communion. You can pray to Me as an infant as well, and you can have a display of My crib scene in your prayer room to share all year long. Your little sanctuary light in your prayer room can represent this Light of My angels that are constantly singing My praises. Rejoice with My angels and give thanks and praise to Me for becoming your Redeemer and Savior."*

Monday, January 2, 2006: (St. Basil & St. Gregory)

At Holy Name after Communion I could see into a prison cell and there were posts where Christians were being tortured to death. Jesus said: *"My people, this vision of Christians being tortured to death is going on today and will be going on during the tribulation. Some will be martyred for My Name's sake, while others will be saved at My refuges. There is a description in Mark 13:9,12-13 of the tribulation time.* 'But be on your guard. For they will deliver you up to councils, and you will be beaten in synagogues, and you will stand before governors and kings for my sake, for a witness to them.' 'And brother will hand over brother to death, and the father his child; children will rise up against parents and put them to death. And you will be hated by all for my name's sake; but he who has persevered to the end, will be saved.' *Everyone living at that time will have to suffer through the tribulation. Only by My grace and the help of your guardian angel will you be able to endure it. I will give you what to say at that time by the power of the Holy Spirit. Do not be afraid, but have faith and confidence that My angels will protect you at My refuges where you will be led and taken care of. Those, who are martyred, will become instant saints in heaven. Those, who endure this trial, will be living saints to endure this purgatory on earth, and will be rewarded in My Era of Peace and later in heaven."*

Later, at St. Cecilia's tabernacle I could see a beautiful statue and it became caked with dust and ash, and it looked ugly. Then I saw a great darkness with a great wind as embers of light were streaming by me. The last scene in daylight showed a great mudslide overflow a dam, and water came rushing over a city in torrents. It appeared that a pyroclastic flow came rushing out of a large volcano. Jesus said: *"My people, I have told you that you will be seeing more disasters of large proportions. This great volcanic explosion will send great amounts of dust and ash into the air and could affect the world's weather and your crops. This will be another contributor to a world famine that could come upon you quickly. The food, that I asked you to set aside, will be needed at this time. I will multiply your food so you can distribute it to many in need of being saved from starvation. The miracles of multiplication and healing will contribute greatly in saving many souls that otherwise might have been lost. Many of these disasters will confound the proud and the powerful as they will lose the possessions that they were relying on. Better to trust in My help with My angels, and you will have nothing to fear."*

Tuesday, January 3, 2006: (Holy Name of (Jesus))

At Holy Name after Communion I could see a pool of water and the rock around the edges had been worn away over the years. Jesus said: *"My people, you have read of My Baptism by St. John the Baptist in the Jordan River as in the Gospel reading. This is one of the Scriptural accounts of the appearance of the Blessed Trinity for all to see and hear.* (Matt. 3:21-22) 'Now it came to pass when all the people had been baptized, Jesus also having been baptized and being in prayer, that heaven was opened, and the Holy Spirit descended upon Him in bodily form as a dove, and a voice from heaven 'Thou are My beloved Son, in Thee I am well pleased." *The voice from heaven was My heavenly Father, and from this you have been given the Sign of the Cross and the Glory Be prayers that honor the Blessed Trinity. The vision of the pool of water represents the Baptism of the people into My faith community. You have your sins washed away symbolically with water, but in reality your souls are cleansed by My sacrificial Blood on the cross. The many years of wear on the stone around the pool represents how many years ago this happened and how many have been baptized in My Name since that time. You are blessed with this Sign of the Cross at birth and as you are buried at your funeral."*

Later, at St. Theodore's Adoration I could see a large bell which was symbolic of freedom and bringing in the new year. Jesus said: *"My people, in America you have taken your freedoms for granted, yet in communist countries there is still slave labor and a suppression of expressing religious beliefs. Even though you have supposed freedom of religion, your judges are trying to restrict what you can say about God or even pray in public. Many things as Bibles, the Ten Commandments, crucifixes, and Nativity scenes are being forbidden in public places. My people still need to express their love for Me and your neighbor in any way that you see fit. Do not be afraid to evangelize souls and use these things to show your belief in Me. If you witness to My Name in public, I will witness for you before My heavenly Father."*

Wednesday, January 4, 2006: (Elizabeth Ann Seton)
At Holy Name after Communion I could see a large shaft going down into the ground as a coal mine. Jesus said: *"My people, in the mining explosion in West Virginia it was unfortunate that the news of the fate of the miners killed was not accurate. Many were praying for miracles, but the final truth brought sadness again. You have seen similar accidents in America and other countries. Safety in these dangerous conditions is not always easy when you are dealing with potentially explosive mixtures in the air underground. Possibly better working conditions might result from this accident and violations should be corrected before it could cause any more fatalities. The general public is not aware of how much coal is used by your factories, and how many other mines might have similar problems. Pray for all of your miners and their safety as*

they risk their lives to bring you your sources of fuel."

Later, at St. Theodore's Adoration I could see a white room in a hospital emergency where nurses and doctors were waiting to treat the miners, but they were not needed. Jesus said: *"My people, this vision is all about the preparations that were made at the hospital for live miners, but there was only one that lived. The other minors instead will be sent to the coroner at the morgue for autopsies. More focus has been on the mistaken communications that were too premature and too optimistic before the real facts were known. The explosion and carbon monoxide have taken their toll, and many families were not only upset with the deaths, but also with the false hopes that were given. Many across your nation have sympathized with the families, and some strong investigations will be going on for all mines with violations of any kind. Governments of various levels may be called on to provide aid to the families who have lost their wage earners. Pray for these families in their grief and for their immediate needs."*

Thursday, January 5, 2006: (Dick Mauer's funeral Mass)

At St. Thomas the Apostle after Communion I had a vision of the casket with Dick and it was a new beginning for his life after death. Jesus said: *"My people, it is not easy to suffer the loss of a father and grandfather in a large family. Dick's life was a beautiful expression of care for all of those that he tried to help in life. He helped people in various skills that he had and he truly used his gifts for everyone. He had a great love for Me and My Blessed Mother. He loved to be with Me at Adoration and he spread devotion for My Blessed Mother's Rosary to all who would listen and take a rosary. He spread his faith values through all of his family and to those who would listen to his advice. He is a model for all parents to share the faith with their children. He was a very active witness in what he believed in Me, and many will miss his pleasant words of encouragement. His new beginning after death will allow him to pray for all of his living family and join with his deceased family members. Rejoice in celebrating this man's gift of life to all of you."*

Later, at the prayer group at Holy Name Adoration I could see a large slab of rock and there were demonic symbols and idols being worshiped by those who love Satan. Jesus said: *"My people, I am warning My faithful to avoid movies about witchcraft and TV programs about witches.*

There are various evil influences even in simple things as tarot cards, astrology and Quija boards. Drugs and various music can also lead people to openings to demon possessions or obsessions. I cast many demons out of people as you have read of My miracles. There are even more demon possessed people now, but they are hidden by certain mental illnesses. There are exorcist priests and deliverance people who are still casting out demons, but this takes graces of preparation and prayer in My Name. Carry your blessed sacramentals for protection from evil people and the demons. Trust in My protection and I will be with you with power greater than any demon."

I could see some small coal cars with workers in a mine. Jesus said: *"My people, there are many jobs in your work force that live with daily dangers. Some work in mines, some in chemical plants, steel mills or making pesticides or other poisons. This latest mining incident points out how important it is to stress safety in every work place. At times people are complacent with these everyday dangers, but when people are injured or killed, then you realize how you have to be alert to accidents at all times. Pray for your workers and employers to take care of safe working conditions and remove any unnecessary risks."*

I could see some flooding in California and fires in Texas and Oklahoma. Jesus said: *"My people, you have only just entered this new year and already you are being tested by flooding, fires, and ice storms. I am telling you that this year will again see great trials with destruction and great loss of life. There are so many ways that natural destruction can bring you to your knees. Heavy rains in California have caused some major flooding with some loss of life. Fires in Texas and Oklahoma have burned many dwellings. Twelve miners have lost their lives from a mine explosion. Earthquakes and volcanoes are continuing and will again take more life and a loss of homes. Your storms continue to destroy structures and kill people in hurricanes and tornadoes. See all of these signs increasing in numbers and intensity as a warning of the coming tribulation. Call on Me in prayer for My protection and a safe shelter."*

I could see faithful Christians coming together to help each other through the many trials of life. Jesus said: *"My people, Christians are speaking out more about 'Merry Christmas' even when it may not be politically correct for some. In many of these disasters you are seeing Good Samaritans coming forth with substantial donations and help to rebuild the homes lost by the hurricanes. It is one thing to talk about love and charity, but it is even more meaningful to reach out and help someone in need by donating your time, talent, and treasure. I provide these opportunities to gain grace, so do not pass them up just for your own comfort and convenience. Your reward will be great in heaven for all that you can do to help My little ones."*

I could see some people looking around the corner of a building to see what was coming. Jesus said: *"My people, many of your economists like to make educated predictions of how your economy will perform in the next years. Some are concerned about interest rates rising, increasing fuel costs, worsening deficits, or more layoffs in manufacturing. All of these things can influence your jobs and finances, but do not just be concerned about physical trials because you can call on My help in all that you do. Trust in Me to lead you on the right path to heaven so you can guard your souls against the evil ones and their temptations."*

I could see some people concerned about their outward appearance and their new resolutions to change. Jesus said: *"My people, there are those working on their diets to get their bodies in shape with additional exercise. Remember how I suggested that improving your inner appearance is of even more importance to your soul. Some of your fasting can serve a double purpose of improving your weight and developing self-control to avoid falling into sin. You are called to take care of your body and not to overindulge in eating, drinking, smoking, or too many drugs and medications. By making your new resolutions and calling on My help, you can work to eliminate some of your bad habits and move closer to holiness."*

I could see a place in front of an Adoration room where people sign their names and time of Adoration. Jesus said: *"My people, you may be fortunate to know of some places of Adoration or open churches where you can visit Me in My Blessed Sacrament. I give all of you an opportunity to show your love for Me by coming to give Me praise and worship in My consecrated Host. As you look upon My Host, you can tell Me your troubles and ask Me to help lighten your heavy burdens in life. My adorers are always special to Me and you will be blessed by My graces for every visit that you make to see Me. Give yourself some silent time with Me and your heart will be enriched with My Word and My love."*

Friday, January 6, 2006:

At St. John the Evangelist after Communion I could see some trash on the road and snow was coming down, and an eye was looking through all of this. Jesus said: *"My people, as you look out into this world, the trash in the vision is the sin and immorality of the people that you see in filthy movies, prostitution, homosexual parades, and adult bookshops. The blizzard of snow represents all the news and activities going on around you all of the time. My advice is to make some quiet time for yourself in prayer every day, especially in front of Me in Adoration, or in My tabernacle. If you do not shut off your TV and radio for a time, you cannot think straight with all of this clutter going on all of the time. The world is full of temptations and distractions that can keep you busy and steal away any time for your prayer life. It is up to you to make time so you can get off the world's merry-go-around and have some true peace and rest with your Lord. The world is full of stress, and you need to rest your mind and soul, just as you take time at night to sleep and rest your body. This spiritual refreshment with Me will give you the grace and endurance to withstand all of the trials of this evil age."*

Later, at St. Theodore's tabernacle, I could see a night scene of a water fountain, and on the top of a tall building there were communication antennas with fireworks going off above them. Jesus said: *"My people, you are starting another year with celebrations, but the one world people are using their surveillance cameras and phone taps to strip more of your freedoms in the name of security. This year your passports will need to have smart cards with digital pictures and biometrics of your fingerprints or iris scans. Your driver's licenses will be required to have smart cards as well over the next few years. These people want to control your buying and selling and there will be reprisals for those who do not go along with their new world order. Eventually, punishments could be a loss of your bank accounts or prison in a detention center. As the evil ones try to force chips in the hand, My faithful should refuse chips in the body even if they threaten to kill you. Chips in the body could be used to control your mind and eventually your soul through worshiping the Antichrist. Call on My help and My angels will lead you to My refuges before they can come to your house to force chips in the body on you. Even if you give up everything, I will supply you with water, food, and shelter at My refuges. Have faith and trust in Me that My power will vanquish these evil ones and I will lead you into My Era of Peace."*

Saturday, January 7, 2006: (Cana Gospel)
    At St. John the Evangelist after Communion I could see the outline of our Blessed Mother as she cares for her children. Jesus said: *"My people, in this vision of My Blessed Mother she is always a caring person as in the Gospel when she advised Me of the wine running out at Cana. My compassion reached out to help the bride and groom as well as answering My Blessed Mother's request. She is your mother also as she watches over her children with her mantle of protection. This situation was a teaching moment in both honoring marriage as a sacrament with*

Josyp Terelya

My first miracle, and teaching My apostles of My powers as the Son of God in performing such miracles. The added touch of My mercy was that this new wine was not just ordinary, but it was of excellent quality that even the head waiter noticed. This should also be a lesson to My faithful when you are teaching people about the faith, that you can use many such incidents as teaching moments and examples of My love."

Later, at St. Cecilia's tabernacle I could see a long boom with a large microphone at the end of it and it was listening to people's conversations. Jesus said: *"My people, you have read of the controversy of dodging the law to have phone taps on people without a warrant. The real truth is that your government is listening to every communication for words about terrorism. In addition they are profiling your citizens to see if they would give the one world people trouble in establishing their new world order. If you are strong about your freedoms or are religious, they are placing you on lists to be exterminated or placed in detention centers. Call on Me in prayer and you will be protected at My refuges. The evil ones will be persecuting you for your beliefs which are contrary to the Antichrist's plans. Stay true to your faith and refuse to use the microchips that could control your minds if you place them in your body. I will defeat the evil ones and cast them into hell, but My faithful will be made ready for My Era of Peace after I renew the earth. Rejoice when I come, for your joy with Me will be great both on earth and in heaven."*

Sunday, January 8, 2006: (The Epiphany)

At Holy Name after Communion I could see the Light shining from Jesus as in the Warning and at death. Jesus said: *"My people, there is more to My coming than a miraculous star. This Light of My appearance in the vision is the same Light that you will be drawn to at your Warning experience, and at your death. My mere Presence gives Light to the world and you can see a glimmer of My Presence in every person on earth. St. John, the apostle and evangelist, speaks of My Light in the beginning of his Gospel.* (John 1:4-5) *'In Him was life, and the life was the Light of men. And the Light shines in the darkness; and the darkness grasped it not.' Even though the Pharisees tried to snuff out My message by killing Me, they were confounded by My Resurrection, and My Church continues to spread My message even until now. All of My faithful have been given a gift of faith and a part of My Light that you need to share with all nations from the rooftops. Just as the Magi brought their gifts, you can also bring Me both your physical and spiritual gifts through your daily consecration. Believe in My message of Light and follow Me throughout all of your life."*

Monday, January 9, 2006: (Baptism of (Jesus))

At Holy Name after Communion I could see a split in a seat and then it was sewn up and it looked as good as new. Jesus said: *"My people, since I have come into the world to die for you, you are all baptized in the Spirit and not just by water alone. When the Holy Spirit is in you, you will be inspired to spread the faith to all people. This vision of a divided seat being sewn together is a sign that I want all of My people to be peacemakers. The evil one has planted seeds of division all over, but you are called to heal divisions and unrest among families, and bring My peace into their souls. Holding grudges and bitterness is the opposite of the love that I want you to spread among your people. Peace is far better than wars and continual hate. Find ways to work out your differences instead of following the evil one in perpetual wars. All wars are a failure in relations, and they will not be solutions, but become more of the problem. Live in My peace and love, or you will destroy yourselves with your pride and greed."*

Later, at St. Theodore's tabernacle I could look down a dark well and someone was being pulled up to be saved. Then I saw someone traveling through a horizontal tunnel on a walkway, but the sides moved around ever faster. Jesus said: *"My people, this vision of being saved in a deep well is how some people see the need for the forgiveness of their sins. The more you dwell on your sins, the more sorry you are for having offended God. The rotating tunnel gives you a feeling of lost balance and disorientation. When you are going through the tunnel of your Warning experience, you will be outside of your body and the only things with you will be your good and bad actions of your life. All of your possessions and earthly comforts will be stripped from you, and you will be traveling in the spirit world. I will review all of your life's actions before you, and you will see how they affected other people and how they saw you. A fair judgment will be pronounced on you to go to heaven, purgatory, or hell. You will see a vision of where you would be judged, but you will also be put back into your body with a second chance to change your life. Call on My help because this experience will be a great test of your faith for everyone at the same time. Those, who are faithful to Me, will receive protection and a reward in My Era of Peace. Those, who reject Me in favor of the Antichrist, will be thrown into the fires of Gehenna forever."*

Tuesday, January 10, 2006:

At Holy Name after Communion I could see someone in a boat going down a small stream with large walls on either side as in a deep ravine. Jesus said: *"My people, during life, you have many obstacles to overcome that may seem insurmountable as these steep cliffs in the vision. In the reading Hannah's barrenness seemed to her an impossible dream to conceive a son. Yet, she was asking Me in prayer to answer her intention. Her faith enabled her to be answered with her son, Samuel. I know all of your problems and concerns, but it is your persistence and faith in your prayers that can overcome mountains. I told My apostles if they had the faith as small as a mustard seed, that they could do great things beyond their dreams. This is the lesson for all of My faithful that with Me all things are possible. Pray the most for intentions that are the best for your soul and others, and you will be favored in time."*

Later, at St. Theodore's Adoration I could see a coal furnace being used to generate heat for a building. Jesus said: *"My people, after your hurricanes affected your Gulf Coast supplies of oil and natural gas, you have seen spikes in your fuel costs for your cars and your homes. This experience and coal mine explosions are again showing you how vulnerable your fuel supplies are. The cheapest natural resources are fossil fuels which are being used for your energy sources. Harnessing sun, wind, and nuclear power are other alternatives, as well as hydrogen and ethanol. It may take more research to use recyclable fuels, but each fuel has its dangers and problems to use. Production of carbon dioxide from fossil fuels is also causing other problems in your environment. Price, convenience, and soon environment are the driving forces in why man chooses different fuels. Pray for your fuel companies and your governments to make the right choices so everyone can live in a world that you can hand on to your children without major disasters."*

Wednesday, January 11, 2006:

At St. John the Evangelist after Communion I was allowed to see an ugly looking demon and how they are more present in people than one would think by outward appearances. Jesus said: *"My people, you are seeing in the Gospel how I healed diseases and cast demons out of people. The plural of more than one demon means that it was not uncommon that people had either one or more demons. I have warned you that in this evil age there are also many demons of influence either attached to people or fully possessed in people. You cannot always tell of this possession because these demons can hide their presence and the person appears normal. Some mental illnesses are associated with demons, but demons also are attached to addicted people. Sometimes people invite demons in through seances, witchcraft, drugs, New Age worship of idols, Ouija boards, and Eastern Meditations as Yoga and Reiki exercises. These exercises are worship to various deities of the various hand and body positions. Look at the source of power being invoked, and if they are not calling in My Name, then they are inviting evil spirits. To battle these evil spirits you must protect yourself with holy water, blessed salt, Benedictine blessed crosses containing exorcism medals of St. Benedict, and other blessed sacramentals. Praying the St. Michael Prayer and shaking holy water or blessed salt on possessed people can free some demons. It is best for exorcism to have a priest carry out such a blessing of deliverance, but in the absence of a priest, one can call these demons out in My Name to the foot of the cross and never to return. When you see strange behavior, a rejection of crosses and holy things, expressions of hate, or unusual coldness, these are signs as you know of demonic presence. Remember that My power is greater than the demons and you can call on My power to release people of the demons. The devil and the evil spirits are real entities that have as their one goal to steal your soul from Me to bring it to hell. So look to the Light in Me and I will protect you from any darkness of the evil ones. Have faith and fear no evil because with Me all things are possible."*

Later, at St. Theodore's Adoration I could see a room that had just been refurbished with a new floor, painted walls, new light fixtures, and new furniture. Jesus said: *"My people, at times you are tired of looking at the same things in your rooms. You may have an inspiration to improve the appearance of some old things in your rooms. By changing a little bit at a time you can minimize the cost of each change. Your spiritual life can also get old with time, if you are not thinking of how to improve it. You all are striving for perfection, so there is always room for improvement. Try to make your path to heaven as short as pos-*

sible without so many detours. Work at ways in your new resolutions to come closer to Me in prayer and do not let yourself be so distracted with worldly things. Strive to become holy and avoid occasions of sin that could lead you astray. Once you have made some improvements in your life, then you can compare now with your past efforts. Live to love Me and your neighbor more, and you will be contributing more to peace in the world."

Thursday, January 12, 2006:
At St. John the Evangelist after Communion I could see a newly married couple walking through a large wedding ring. Jesus said: *"My people, I have spoken to you many times that My Church is like a bride and I am the Groom, as I am inviting you all to My Wedding Feast in heaven. This vision of a newly married couple passing through a large wedding ring represents the contract or covenant made between the man and wife to be faithful to each other. This sacrament of Matrimony protects them from any sin of fornication and keeps them pure. In the same way My followers receive Baptism, and Confession when needed, to make a contract of fidelity with Me that you will be faithful to My Commandments. My sacramental grace will keep you pure and strengthen you against sin. Today's Gospel speaks of a healing of leprosy, but I healed the souls as well from their sins at the same time. A healing of souls is far more important for your eternal life than a temporary healing of pain in this short life on earth. Even though you pray for physical healing for people's diseases and pain, it is even better to pray for people to be open to Confession that can heal their soul."*

Later, at the prayer group at Holy Name Adoration I called on my son, David, and I was shown his grave that we visited yesterday on the anniversary of his death. David said: *"My dear father, I am happy that you continue to remember me during your prayers and when you can visit my grave site. I come to you more on the anniversary of my death because it is a birthday into the spirit world. I continue to pray for my parents, my sisters, and their children in all of your trials. The letter that you received is a blessing and an answer to your prayer to me as intercessor. You have had several prayers answered through my intercession, so continue your intentions because Jesus listens to his little ones."*

Note: Virginia was 46 years old, and she had no children and four miscarriages. Since it was the 23rd anniversary of our infant son, David's death, I decided to pray to him to intercede for them to have a child. James was born exactly nine months later on October 11th. This was the letter with a picture of the baby.

I could see flames of houses burning and brush burning on the plains of Texas. Jesus said: *"My people, you have seen fires out West during the summer, but these new outbreaks are unusual in your winter season. You are experiencing some unusually warm weather all over your country and you are realizing that your weather patterns are changing dramatically. These dry conditions in Texas have touched off fires that have taken you by surprise. See that such changes are going to be more frequent as a result of man's influences on his environment."*

I could see sores and disease among the people in Turkey. Jesus said: *"My people, there has been an unusual outbreak of bird flu among the chickens that the people are growing. Some are claiming migratory birds are spreading this flu, but there are some man-made causes that have not been revealed. Those people, who have come in contact with the diseased birds, are the ones who have contracted bird flu and a fair percentage have died. Some have tried to contain this spread by killing the chickens. Getting vaccines and antibiotics to these remote countries has not been very successful. Pray that this disease is contained and that it does not spread between humans."*

I could see some beautifully-colored aurora borealis in the sky and they became very brilliant and started spreading further south than usual. Jesus said: *"My people, this vision of Northern Lights is not unusual because it comes from the sun's constant bombardment of your atmosphere with particles that ionize the molecules releasing colorful displays. It is the polar effects of the earth that only allow these entries at the North and South poles. As the magnetic poles change and lessen in charge, you will be seeing these unusual displays moving further south in your Northern skies. Again this is another sign of the changes in the earth that are preparing you for the end days."*

I could still see the debris left from many of the summer hurricanes, and there were some dark clouds over this area. Jesus said: *"My people, these dark clouds over the areas destroyed by the hurricanes represent the residual evil that hovers over these people trying to rebuild their places of sin. Many people have not returned, and there are still health hazards in the tainted water and mold-infested debris. These people have yet to realize that it was their sins that brought this destruction upon them. Money from governments and aid organizations has been slow in coming to repair all of this damage. There are still lingering doubts whether these levees will stand up to future storms. Pray that these people will see the light and change their sinful ways."*

I could see the committee room where the current Supreme Court candidate was being reviewed. Jesus said: *"My people, those people, who want to keep your abortion rulings unchanged, are greatly concerned about any conservative justice being added to the court. Your country is being given another opportunity to possibly change the makeup of your Supreme Court so that a new decision could be made against your current abortion laws. Unless you change your abortion stand, you will bring more chastisements against you and you will be brought to your knees by natural disasters."*

I could see a nuclear symbol standing over Iran. Jesus said: *"My people, you are seeing Iran fanning the flames of a future confrontation with Israel and possibly other Western countries. Removing UN seals and extending their nuclear plans for making bomb materials has many countries concerned about nuclear weapons in the hands of Muslim extremists. This could present a new source of war if these countries take any further action. Continue to pray for peace in the Middle East or you could possibly see nuclear explosions, or a possible world war over oil and the Arab countries."*

Friday, January 13, 2006:

At St. John the Evangelist after Communion I could see a great wall of stone and on it was displayed a large image of the beast, the Antichrist. Jesus said: *"My people, you have heard the account in the first reading how the Jewish people demanded Samuel to give them a king to lead them in battle against their enemies. Samuel warned them that they would be giving up some freedoms for what they thought was security. In your government today, again the people are desiring security from terrorists, but when you see invasions of your privacy in all of your communications, there are second thoughts about what freedoms are being given up. This loss of your freedoms will be extended further when you will be forced to have smart cards in your driver's licenses and passports. The vision of the beast is even another example of when security, financial hard times, wars, and famines will occur. Then there will be a call for a world leader of peace in the Antichrist. But quickly he will become a tyrant once in control, and he will demand that everyone has to worship him, take his microchips in the body, and post his picture all over, even on your TVs. Refuse to worship this Antichrist and refuse his chips in your body. Instead, call on Me in prayer for protection at My refuges where My angels will provide for all of your needs."*

Later, at St. Theodore's tabernacle I could see the ceiling of the stars in the church over the stone of the Agony in the Garden at Gethsemene. Jesus said: *"My people, this scene of My Agony in the Garden of Gethsemene, where I sweated drops of blood, was My humanity struggling with My imminent death. The quotation in Matthew shows My humanity in asking My cup to be taken away, but My Spirit followed the will of My Father.* (Matt. 26:39) 'He advanced a little and fell prostrate in prayer, saying, 'My Father, if it is possible, let this cup pass from Me; yet, not as I will, but as you will." *In the same way each of you have been given a particular mission to accomplish here on the earth. The more you deny this mission, the harder it will be to carry it out. If you call on Me to help you discern your mission, then it will be made clearer to you what that mission is. Most of My missions are many times in opposition to what your earthly comforts desire. You may be tested at various levels, much like I was in My Agony in the Garden. Once you understand your mission, it may be difficult to carry it out, or you may even endanger your life in the process. You have seen many courageous saints die a martyr's death than deny their faith in My Name. You could be tested as a dry martyr without being killed, or you may have to be strong as I died for you. My martyrs became instant saints and My angels helped them to bear the pain of their death. Trust in Me and have faith, even if you are tested with martyrdom."*

Saturday, January 14, 2006:

At St. John the Evangelist after Communion I could see someone sobbing tears of sorrow as they prepared for Confession in church. Jesus said: *"My people, there are many sinners who are sick with grief over the guilt of their sins. Some have developed serious problems in their stomachs or in mental illnesses from this guilt. When you know that you have done something wrong, there is a desire to lift this guilt of sin from your mind. This is why I have given you My sacrament of*

Reconciliation. In the Gospel call of Levi, the tax collector, I answered the Scribes and Pharisees who criticized My eating with sinners. (Mark 2:17) 'It is not the healthy who need a physician, but they who are sick. For I have not come to call the just, but sinners.' *If people are really truthful with themselves, they will have to admit that they are sinners and are not yet perfected. So everyone is included as a sinner, but those, who think that they are better than others, may not wish to admit their failings. It is those, who seek to be forgiven, that I seek out to forgive and help. Those, who reject Me and do not seek forgiveness, are too full of pride and are on the broad road to hell. So keep humble by coming to Me and following Me in My Commandments, and you will be on the narrow road to heaven."*

Later, at St. Theodore's tabernacle I could see a roster list for a team on the wall of a football stadium. Jesus said: *"My people, when a coach prepares his football team for a hard game, he takes great care in choosing what players to put on his team, and care in training them as well. My people face a daily battle of good and evil every day in your actions. Again you always have to make the right choices and decide whose team that you are going to be on. If you choose to follow Me and My Commandments, you can call on My help in prayer and also My angels, and all the saints. Do not think that you have to enter this battle all alone. You need to plan your day around how best to serve Me in your mission. Those, who choose to follow Satan and the evil ones, are choosing the wrong team because they will be defeated in the end. The evil demons and those who work with them, will be against you, so you know what you are up against and who you can rely on to help you. Have faith in My power because it is greater than all of the evil ones put together. You may see setbacks in various battles, but you know that I will be victorious in winning the war. Focus on My love and peace as you struggle each day to be My worthy servant. At the judgment you will be rewarded for choosing the right team and fighting the good fight for the faith."*

Sunday, January 15, 2006: (Samuel's calling)
At Holy Name after Communion I could see a satellite being sent to view some distant planets and moons. Jesus said: *"My people, man has been in a constant search to learn more about his neighboring planets and any information about the formation of the universe. Most of sci-*

ence is about measurements and observations of how things of the world interact with one another. There are some who do not want to believe in the creation of the universe by God, and are still thinking up theories to explain things. For those, who do believe in creation, they can see the parallel of the sun and the planets on a macro scale, and protons circled by electrons on the micro scale. The order and beauty of the universe had to come from God, rather than out of chaos. Man's real search for truth should start with Me because you all are My creatures, and you need to give Me praise and glory in thanksgiving for all that I have given you. So when Samuel responds: 'Speak Lord, for your servant is listening.' This is the same response that I am looking for from each soul. My prophets and messengers have been given special gifts so that they can share My words with everyone. Now that you read their words of Mine in Scripture, there is no excuse for not listening and following My Commandments."

Monday, January 16, 2006:

At St. John the Evangelist after Communion I could see tracks from snow plows and snow as high as telephone wires. Jesus said: *"My people, you have seen a mild winter up until now. Soon you will be seeing considerably heavy snow bands where it is cold enough to snow. With enough snow you could see traffic problems both on the ground and in the air. The snow plows will again be called out and you will be spending more time cleaning off your cars and driveways. Your weather problems and natural disasters will continue to harass you as one event will happen after another. Pray for My help to endure all that will be going on."*

Later, at St. Theodore's tabernacle I could see a conveyor belt and there were pills stuck in the joints where a company was disposing of outdated pills or pills that had to be taken off the market. Jesus said: *"My people, there is a lot of manipulation and misrepresentation of the facts going on in pharmaceutical drug companies. Some companies know their product has bad side effects, yet they still sell them until the public complains with lawsuits. Some drugs are diluted or exchanged with generic ones to make more money. Prices between different countries are examples of how over priced your drugs are in America. New expensive drugs are encouraged among doctors, even when older generic drugs do just as well. The drug business is worth so much money, that it lends itself to corruption at all levels. People's poor diets and eating habits have created many sick people. Environmental pollution and adulterated foods are another reason that you are seeing so many diseases and cancer. It is unfortunate that a steady diet of these drugs are also causing liver and kidney problems that can even lead to people's death. All of man's medicines have side effects because they are unnatural and are not made for the balance of nature. Herbs and vitamins are better cures in the long run, but because they are cheap, the medical profession even frowns on alternative cures. Natural means for cures are far better for your health and the long term healing of the body. Pray that your doctors and drug companies will provide you with the truth, and not just another means to make them money."*

Tuesday, January 17, 2006: (St. Anthony of the Desert)
At Holy Name after Communion I could see someone loading a ballistic missile into a silo in Iran. Jesus said: *"My people, there is great concern among the countries in Europe and Asia over the proliferation of nuclear armaments, especially in Iran among Muslim extremists. The latest talk of Iran about Armageddon and destroying Israel is further raising the specter of possible war in the Middle East. Such talk could incite Israel into attacking Iran to try and destroy these facilities of secret enrichment of nuclear materials. Some countries are willing to sell nuclear plant materials to Iran, but not weapon's grade fuel. The vision of loading a missile into a silo represents Iran's desire for launching vehicles for their future weapons. UN meetings will be looking into this new threat, but Iran is still moving ahead with its weapon's research program. Iran and North Korea are both becoming potential problems for the world in their threat to use nuclear weapons for blackmail or to destroy their enemies. The evil ones are trying to start world wars, but I encourage My faithful to pray for peace and fair compromise. Love and peace are more desirable than hate and war. Strive to love everyone and be peacemakers instead of making war."*

Later, at St. Theodore's Adoration I could see children's toys sitting on a black plastic, and then I could see a black tunnel heading toward the Light. Jesus said: *"My people, these children's toys and the black tunnel represent how you will be taken back through your childhood again as you are focused on My Light. You will have a new perspective of how your body developed and aged over the years. You will also see how your spiritual faith developed and how you have been down some detours, and brought back to the right path. The years have slipped past you very quickly, and you will see how much you have matured in your faith from the learning from your mistakes. Look for good examples in people around you so you can improve in your holiness. Your whole life is a preparation for your death, and how you can perfect yourself for entry into the spirit world. This coming Warning experience will be a great mercy for people to see the need to change their lives to please Me more in worship with less influence from the world. Follow My directions in the Bible on how to lead a holy and humble life, so you will be more pure and ready for heaven when I call you home. Seek the forgiveness of your sins in Confession and follow this Light to be with your Savior. Help others in their faith, and be prepared to lead sinners to Confession after their Warning experience."*

Wednesday, January 18, 2006:

At St. John the Evangelist after Communion I could see water running over a newly formed cliff from a major earthquake fault. Jesus said: *"My people, you have seen mountain ranges form when one plate either slips up or down, or if one plate folds under another. This vision of a newly formed cliff with water flowing over it represents some major earthquakes that would have to occur to form such a ridge. The last major earthquake has shown a major ridge that formed underwater and it was the cause of so much water to be displaced in the formation of the tsunami. This ridge formation could also happen above ground, or at a coastline. Your earthquake and volcanic activity have been on the increase. Such a major earthquake could even change the geography of an impacted area. These events go on over the years, but recent earthquakes are getting more intense and more frequent giving you another sign of the end times."*

Later, at St. Theodore's Adoration I could see some signs still on the ground in New Orleans that have not been put up on their stands. Jesus said: *"My people, there has been some cleanup of the streets in New Orleans, but there is still a lot of damage and debris that has not been touched. Those people of little means do not have the money to rebuild their houses unless money comes from various levels of government. Others, who have received insurance money, may have chosen to build elsewhere after seeing the levees fail twice with Katrina and Rita. I have mentioned before that this destruction was striking where there were rampant sexual sins and voodoo going on. If these houses of prostitution and homosexual parades continue to defy My Commandments in their rebuilding, you could see further storms punish this area again. Those, who openly flaunt their sinful activity in My face, can expect swift justice from My righteous wrath. It is unfortunate that some good people have been suffering along with the evil people, but it may be a lesson to avoid living in these areas that make money on sinful activity."*

Thursday, January 19, 2006:

At St. John the Evangelist after Communion I could see a light fixture as a headlight of a car at night. Jesus said: *"My people, the psalm at Mass speaks of trusting in Me and to have no fear. There are various fears that you have in life and one of them is darkness, when you cannot see things. Darkness causes you to be disoriented without a sense of direction. This is why you put on your headlights on your car, as in the vision, to see at night and on dark cloudy days. At night you put on lights both inside and outside of your house to see where you are going. There is also a spiritual darkness or darkness of the soul when you are without your God and you are searching for direction in your life. I am that Light that dispels the darkness of evil and all of your sins. You come to Me for love, for forgiveness, and for direction in how to gain heaven. Without My help your existence would cease, and without My grace, you cannot accomplish anything. It is by My grace that you can live and use your talents to complete the mission that I have set before you. You may fear death or the demons, but do not worry or be afraid because if you have Me with you, you do not need anything else. Call on My help whenever you are threatened, and I will be at your side. I always see your needs, so I can be there for you, but you must have trust and faith in My power. The one, who has no fear, is the one who truly believes in My help. Do not even be afraid of death because it is part of this life and is required before you can enter heaven. It is proper to guard your body from dangers, but I am the One who calls you home. That is why killing of any kind is very offensive to Me because it violates My laws and My plan for life. Such people, who advocate death, will be held accountable before Me."*

Later, at the prayer group at Holy Name Adoration I could see soldiers, propeller-driven planes, and then modern jets, ballistic missiles, and nuclear weapons. Jesus said: *"My people, you have had a stand off with many nuclear weapons on either side of the cold war for many years. Now the super powers are concerned that Arab militants want to make their own atomic weapons to carry on their war with the West. The Arab countries control a major amount of the world's oil supplies, and they can black mail other nations into supporting their right to make nuclear weapons by threatening to cut off oil supplies. Now more than ever, you need to pray for peace because Iran and North Korea are threatening it by making atomic weapons."*

I could see all of the killing and terrorism going on in Iraq. Jesus said: *"My people, your attacks against Saddam and Osama Bin Laden have been successful initially, but America will not withstand a long drawn out war of attrition because of the cost and the troops lost. This lesson is why it would not be plausible to start even more wars against Iran and North Korea. War possibilities in the Middle East are heating up and countries with nuclear weapons are even threatening the unthinkable of actually using these weapons. Pray that such dramatic loss of life does not happen with the use of nuclear bombs. The more terrorists strike in various countries, killing at random, the more reprisals could be seen against Arabs in general. Pray for My peace and not man's false peace."*

I could see films of Osama Bin Laden as his words were causing fear of more terrorist attacks. Jesus said: *"My people, these latest tapes of the militant terrorist groups are speaking of truce on one hand, but they are inciting a world jihad against America and the Western nations that support Israel on the other hand. The war against terror is accelerating with every killing and every missile attack. By their words, the Arab militants will not have peace until all of the infidels are killed. This means that you will be in constant war without end. Even with these words of war, I still want My people to love everyone and stop the killing."*

I could see people using a church where parts of the roof were missing. Jesus said: *"My people, as time goes on the militant atheists will be trying to destroy My Church. Already some churches are closing because of a priest shortage and scandals in the priesthood. Churches are going to lose their tax exemption when they fight against the social issues that are contrary to your government laws that advocate abor-*

tion and homosexual marriages. Then Christians will be sought out for torture and killing in your detention centers as the Antichrist will come to power. Refuse to approve of man's desire to kill in abortion, euthanasia, and meaningless wars, even if your life is threatened in martyrdom."

I could see businesses and factories in China producing all the world's goods with cheap labor. Jesus said: *"My people, as the latest political dealings are focused on China, Russia, and the Arab countries, your manufacturing leaders are realizing their huge mistake in building up a communist nation that has as its goal world domination. All of your manufacturing and technical skills are migrating to China while America will be left dependent on their factories for everything. Wake up America because you have been sold out by the very businesses that you have started up. Your current industries are losing the current economic war as your weapons become obsolete. If your business leaders do not stop exporting your jobs and manufacturing, then you will become a third world country. Follow My ways even if the worldly are taunting you and killing you. Trust in My protection as I will subdue all of these evil killers."*

I could see America sinking deep into a quagmire of wars and deficits. Jesus said: *"My people, there are those people behind the scenes who are trying to destroy America so the Antichrist could easily come to power. The one world people are controlling your government leaders to cause more deficit prone wars and burdens of debt that will throw you into bankruptcy. Most of your debts come from wars and mandated benefits that could never be all paid for through taxes. When your debts stifle your businesses and people cannot collect their promised benefits, your economy will collapse in chaos and the one world people will declare a martial law takeover. Natural disasters and deficits will be your undoing because you have turned your back against your Master."*

I could see a beautiful glow of Light from the Lord's Real Presence coming from the consecrated Hosts at an underground Mass. Jesus said: *"My people, you are going to be faced with hard times as the tribulation and My Warning come near. The one hope and joy amidst all of these troubling world developments is that I am still present among you in My Blessed Sacrament. No matter how the evil ones will try to destroy My faithful, the gates of hell will never prevail over My faithful remnant in My elect. Even if you must face martyrdom or a difficult life at My refuges, do not be afraid for I will be at your side to protect your souls from the demons. Be true to My Word and you will have your reward with Me in heaven."*

Friday, January 20, 2006:

At St. John the Evangelist after Communion I could look up and I saw faces of those in heaven in a circle looking down on all the evil going on in this world. Jesus said: *"My people, you need to put into perspective the plan of the evil ones for world takeover. The one world people in the masons and other groups have planned the demise of America behind the scenes. They are causing all of your wars and leading your leaders into losing wars that accomplish nothing but ruining your economy by huge war debts and destroying the morale of your people. They only inspire hate between peoples because they profit from wars and see that America can be taken over in your weakness that they will cause. Instead, seek peace and love even your enemies. When they threaten your lives, it will be time to be led to My refuges of protection. I will then destroy these evil killers and thieves and cast their lot into hell. By living a holy, humble, and peaceful life, you will be rewarded in My Era of Peace and in heaven. My power will reign, but you must be patient with this evil age that is under the devil's influence. The power of prayer is much more powerful against evil than all of your physical weapons."*

Later, at St. Theodore's tabernacle I could see a long hallway to a nuclear plant for electricity. Jesus said: *"My people, the militant terrorists are planning attacks to try and shut down America's economy. There are many potential targets, but the two types of targets would be to shut down your power grids and your fuel supplies. Attacks on nuclear power plants would cause problems with radiation leaks as well as power outages. Key points in your grids have shown before how you can be blacked out. Attacks on oil and gasoline pipe lines, as well as natural gas lines could shut down power plants, heating, and travel. Protecting all of these targets from terrorism would be very difficult. The terrorists may cause some damage, but the reprisals against Arab countries could throw the rest of the world into deep fuel shortages that could cause a world recession or a world war. Just as America miscalculated in how to deal with Iraq after the takeover, so the Arab militants may be miscalculating the response to their attacks. This is why My people need to pray more for peace in the world before man in his pride and revenge takes the world to the brink of self-extermination. The use of nuclear weapons are not the plan of the one world people because it would destroy all of their microchips. But in haste and desperation some country with these nuclear weapons could use them in defense. Pray to stop these wars before they get started, or you will see as in Iraq that you cannot finish what you have started. Pray for My peace and for the terrorists to stop their attacks."*

Saturday, January 21, 2006: (St. Agnes)

At St. John the Evangelist after Communion I could see a woman with her hand on a door, and you could see her wearing a wedding ring. Jesus said: *"My people, there are many good women, who are married, that are faithful to their husbands in love and also love their children. I am among those families helping them to ward off many attacks from your evil society. The husband and wife families should be the core of your society where children can grow up in a loving environment of father and mother. There are also other dedicated women, as St. Agnes, who are married to Me in the cloister or various convents. Many communities of nuns have broken down as worldly influences have entered in. Being faithful to your Lord in vows of virginity are becoming rare in your society, but they fulfill a need for prayer that is badly needed in this age of sexual sins and killings. Pray for all women who are struggling in their marriages, single life, and those being faithful to Me as nuns."*

Sunday, January 22, 2006:

At Holy Name after Communion I could see Jesus as an infant at Bethlehem, then as a child teaching in the temple, and finally as an adult teaching and healing. Jesus said: *"My people, every person on earth has a mission that they are called to, and only that unique person has been given the gifts to achieve that mission of theirs. My mission as the Son of God was to give you the Good News of the Kingdom of God, and to redeem mankind of their sins. You, My son, have been called to a unique mission of preparing My people for the end times. You were given the faith through your parents and teachers. You were called to be a daily Communicant and a deacon at one time that your pastor asked you to postpone. Then in Medjugorje you were called to serve*

Me in a special way as one of My messengers. This is also a calling to a humble, prayerful life that I invited you from your working job. Just as I called My apostles from their worldly jobs, so I call people to work for Me in various walks of life besides the priesthood. My priest sons are My special ministers to teach and feed My people with My sacraments. Everyone needs to pray for discernment for knowing your mission and remaining faithful to your call. When you hear My words: 'Follow Me', you are to drop what you are doing and immediately see where I am leading you. This will save your soul for heaven."

Later, at St. Theodore's tabernacle I could see people building new casinos in Las Vegas and in the Southern states. Jesus said: *"My people, more and more gambling casinos are going up in states all over your country as a tourist attraction and a way to make money for states and run down areas. The reason for this extra game building is because they are so profitable for the management. These establishments rig their equipment for generous profits, even when they allow a few wins. It is unfortunate that those, who have gambling addictions, are being encouraged to lose their money in more locations. It is entertainment when you set reasonable amounts to bet, but it can cause financial disaster to families who cannot afford these losses. Those family members, that gamble heavily, should be encouraged by their family to seek counseling at clinics to help people with gambling addictions. Do not let the desire for winning fast money fool you into gambling money that you cannot afford to lose. Even excessive lottery buying can cause problems as well. You do not need gambling in your life to have good entertainment. Pray for those gambling addicts that need help, and discourage these kind of dwellings in your states, towns, or cities."*

Monday, January 23, 2006:

At Holy Name after Communion I could see trumpets celebrating David as King, then heavenly trumpets for Jesus as King on earth. Jesus said: *"My people, there was great rejoicing in Israel when David became king and led his people to victory over the peoples around them. Even the Messiah, that the Israelites awaited, was supposed to be an earthly king and save them from the Romans. When I came and announced that the Kingdom of God was before them, they did not believe that a carpenter could be their king. Even though man did not revel about My kingship, the angels in heaven blew their trumpets in celebration. But My kingship was not of this world. It is in heaven in the spirit world. I gave St. Peter the keys to the Kingdom of heaven as I made him head of My Church. Rejoice, My people, for I, your King, am with you all days, even to the end of time."*

Later, at Our Lady of Lourdes Adoration I could see many crosses standing in front of me and representing the many lives taken by abortion. Jesus said: *"My people, every year, that your country tolerates killing almost half of your unborn infants, is another stake that you place in My suffering Heart. You have some new judges being seated on your Supreme Court that could possibly sway some future decisions in favor of the unborn. If you do not change this decision and precedent of allowing abortions, you will face more disasters and risk the loss of your freedoms. You have seen in your news reports that many Western nations have fertility rates that are not even replacing the deaths of their people. When you kill half of your infants in the womb, you will have less workers to support your Social Security and Medical programs. You are causing financial and spiritual losses among your nations with continued killing in abortion. Some governments are now seeing the errors in birth control and are encouraging women to have more children. Now even nature and your very populations are telling you how evil and wrong it is to kill so many infants. You have favored convenience and comforts over nurturing your children, so now you are reaping the consequences of your sins against My plan for life. Change your laws and decisions that are in favor of abortion before your country falls completely into the hands of the evil ones. America's Judgment Day is near, and the scales of your heavy sins are outweighing your good deeds and prayers. Just as Jonah announced to Nineveh that it would be destroyed if they did not repent, so America also will be destroyed if you do not repent of your abortions."*

Tuesday, January 24, 2006:

At Holy Name after Communion I could see a car driving down a road into a valley. Jesus said: *"My people, this vision of a car driving down into a valley represents another manufacturing area that is losing money and closing factories and cutting 30,000 jobs. Your American companies have a hard time competing with foreign subsidized cars and cheaper labor in other countries. Your government has a free trade policy, that is destroying all of your manufacturing industries because foreign products are not fairly competing. You give tax incentives for sending jobs overseas, and even tax advantages for foreign companies to operate in America. This is not by accident that your government is encouraging the demise of your factories and the loss of middle class wages. It is the goal of the one world people to destroy the middle class so you can easily be controlled in your finances. It is only the rich and large stockholders that profit from shipping your jobs overseas. Even your technology industries are going overseas. Then your main exports will be agricultural and natural resources, leaving you as a third world country and ripe for takeover by the one world people. If your country does not shift to non-oil fuels, stop your deficits and free trade, then there will be no good paying jobs, small taxes, and your government will be bankrupt. In the same way your country's morals are deteriorating faster than your financial demise. America has lost its faith in God and so you will be both spiritually and financially bankrupt on your way to your own destruction."*

Later, at St. Theodore's Adoration I could see people moving about just as chess pieces with little motivation spiritually and a struggle just to survive. Jesus said: *"My people, many of your people do not seem to have too many goals in life more than work and having some entertainment. Those, who understand that this life is just a preparation for the next life, realize that following My plan is the best way to reach eternity in heaven. You are spirit and flesh, but the body will soon die and you will only be left with your spirit. The spirit craves to be with Me and loves Me, while the body wants to be satisfied with worldly comforts and pleasures. In your striving for spiritual perfection, you must be willing to die to self and give up your worldly desires for love of Me and serving Me. Your country's morals are getting worse as you are seeing abortions, bad movies, prostitution, pornography, homosexual marriages, divorces, and fornication in living together. Many of your natural disasters and job losses are a punishment for your many sins. Pray for your people to repent of their sins and lead holier lives so you can stop the spiritual slide in your morals. America has a choice to either improve its morals or go the way of the Roman Empire which was destroyed from within."*

Wednesday, January 25, 2006: (Conversion of St. Paul)

At Holy Name after Communion I could see a long dark pathway and then the Light of Jesus came. Jesus said: *"My people, not everyone has had such a physical manifestation as St. Paul did in his conversion with My Light. This was a special miracle as Saul was changed to Paul. St. Paul became one of My greatest missionaries to inspire My faithful. Converts sometimes have a stronger faith than Catholics from birth because they have made a choice to follow Me. Even baptized Catholics and Christians need to make a personal commitment to serve Me at some point in their lives. I have called many clergy and even lay people to go out and preach My Word so that more souls could be converted to the faith. Some of My chosen prophets and messengers have been given the honor of receiving messages to share My love and peace with everyone. It is unfortunate that even many Catholics do not believe in My Real Presence in My Eucharistic Host. Since the Last Supper, you have heard My words of the Consecration that changes*

bread and wine into My Body and Blood. Some did not understand or wanted to believe that I would give you My Body to eat and My Blood to drink. But then I said further that unless you eat My Body and drink My Blood, you cannot have life in you. (John 6:54,55) 'He who eats My Flesh and drinks My Blood has life everlasting and I will raise him up on the last day.' *There are people who still do not believe that I am really present in My Blessed Sacrament, and to those who did not believe I said:* (John 6:64) 'It is the spirit that gives life; the flesh profits nothing. The words that I have spoken to you are spirit and life.' **This is why My**

Adorers of My Blessed Sacrament are special to Me, because they have taken to heart and truly believe in My Real Presence in My consecrated Host, wherever My Blessed Sacrament is present. Rejoice, that I have given you My very Self to be with you in My Eucharist until I return again."

Later, at St. Theodore's Adoration I could see a wintry scene of snow and ice, and another scene of no snow. Jesus said: *"My people, this winter you have seen hot and cold with a January of a near record high average temperature. Your scientists have determined that 2005 had the highest mean temperature of the world since records were started back in the 1800's. Some have put the cause of a one degree upward shift on increased amounts of carbon dioxide from burning fossil fuels. Still the dramatic shifts in your temperatures are a sign of changing weather patterns that have made your storms more violent than ever. It is hard for man to determine if his pollution and waste streams are affecting the weather and melting the northern ice pack. More studies of these effects might prove to you that man can upset the balance of nature that I established at creation. Pray that you will change your habits so the earth can recover from the damage that you have done to your environment. When I come to vanquish all evil on the earth, I will cast the evil ones into hell, and renew the earth to its former beauty so it is ready for the Era of Peace."*

Thursday, January 26, 2006: (St. Timothy & St. Titus)

At St. John the Evangelist after Communion I could see two floors of a house. The upper floor represented a Christian civilization based on the laws of God. The lower floor represented a pagan civilization that worshiped gods of the earth and was based on man's laws. Jesus said: *"My people, over the years man has seen dark ages and ages of renewal. You are seeing in the readings how I sent out My apostles and deacons to spread My Good News of the Kingdom of God. All but one of My apostles were martyred and many Christians, but My Church has survived. As different civilizations rose and fell, many times new missionaries were sent out to convert the people from their pagan ways. Those civilizations, that deteriorated morally, gradually destroyed themselves. Your country in America was founded on Christian principles, but you have deteriorated in your morals as well. When people turn their backs on Me, then you will reap the consequences of your sins.*

When the family is strong in faith, it has My blessings not to fall into divorce. The children also benefit from a stable, holy environment. It is the responsibility of the parents to pass on this gift of the faith in your teaching and your good example of a good prayer life and regular Mass attendance. It is when you fall away from the faith, that you see more divorce and the children fall away also. Even in a good family environment the children face a lot of distractions from the faith from their friends and worldly attractions. This is why even in America, you have become a mission land because of the immoralities in your society. Continue to pray for souls to repent of their sins, and be converted or renewed in their former faith. Remember that your goal is to spend eternity with Me in heaven because this world is passing away. Only the strong in faith with My help will be the faithful that will make it to heaven."

Later, at the prayer group at Holy Name Adoration I could see Jesus on the cross. Jesus said: *"My people, as you approach Lent in four weeks, it would be a good time to think of some spiritual problem or bad habit that you need to correct. As you meditate on where you need to improve in your spiritual life, you could also think of something that you could give up or do for other people. Making a little act of self-denial, or doing something extra to help people is a beautiful gift to Me if you are sincere in carrying it out through all of Lent."*

I could see several people at a polling place. Jesus said: *"My people, you have seen recent elections among the Palestinians and the people of Iraq. The outcome may not be always to America's liking, but they are choosing their own leaders. In other Arab states power is not always freely chosen. America and other countries are getting bogged down in drawn out wars when you try to force your own way of government on Arab states. There is concern over protecting oil production in the Middle East, but foreign countries should not be dictating who should run their countries. Pray for peace in this area and that nations may find compromises instead of wars that cause destruction."*

I could see some wood structures out in the country where refuges were located. Jesus said: *"My people of America, you have many comforts in your homes, cars, and many electrical devices. Many of your convenient appliances provide for your food production, clothes being washed, and entertainment. At the refuges you will be stripped of your current possessions, but your necessities will be satisfied. This may be a rustic life in more crude facilities, but it will allow you to see what is truly important in this life, and that is your focus on entering heaven."*

I could see some natural gas storage tanks. Jesus said: *"My people, there was initially some concern about a shortage of natural gas and the price rose considerably. Now with your warmer than usual temperatures, you have seen the demand go down as well as the price. There is still more potential for colder weather, but your people have been spared larger bills than they expected. Pray for those people that do not have extra money for higher gas prices."*

I could see a white ornate casket laid out before me. Jesus said: *"My people, today's saints of Timothy and Titus had to struggle during the persecution of the Early Christians. It took courage to follow a new religion led by Me and My disciples. There was always a threat of death for becoming a Christian which is not the case now. A time is coming again when Christians will again risk their lives to worship Me. So be strong in your faith, even if you may be asked to die for your faith."*

I could see the twirling clouds of a hurricane and how people are trying to cope with their losses. Jesus said: *"My people, New Orleans and the Southern States as Mississippi and Florida just received some initial money from your government, but it is not enough to pay for everyone's losses not covered by insurance. This problem of your government finding money to support disasters is not new as with poor funding of the September 11th losses. Your people may have to choose between helping your fellow citizens in their hurricane losses, or continuing to pour money into your endless wars."*

Friday, January 27, 2006:

At St. John the Evangelist after Communion I could see people going down a river on a raft where there were rapids and calm spots. Jesus said: *"My people, this raft traveling down a river with rapids and calm spots is like your life that has troubles and joys. At times you are beset by difficult days that you do not think that you will get through as in high rapids. Then at other times everything is peaceful as the calm of the river. This happens not only with the physical problems of the world, but also with your spiritual life in your sins. In order to return to your spiritual peace, you need frequent Confession, especially for your mortal sins. During life you need to be prepared for the devil's attacks in his temptations for serious and venial sins. You need to focus most on habitual sin so that you can remove any occasions of sin that may make you weak to sin. By focusing on your more frequent sins, you can improve your spiritual life and remove your bonds of control from your sins. Confession cleanses your sins, but you must make a firm commitment not to repeat them. When you try to do everything to please Me, you will see more not to offend Me with your habitual sins."*

Later, at St. Theodore's tabernacle I could see some beautiful ornate outdoor furniture and then inside a house it was filled with pink decorations and the latest electronic appliances. Jesus said: *"My people, it is fortunate if you are able to have a nice home with rich furnishings, but do not let your possessions so consume your time that you have no time left for Me. Do not let anything control you whether it be money, possessions, or addictions. You also should be ready to give up all that you own as you go to My refuges. If you cannot part with your possessions or your money, then you are making these things gods before Me. Be sure to make enough time for Me in your prayers so you have the right priorities. All of these earthly things, that please you today, will become obsolete and useless tomorrow. Eternal life is of more importance than any earthly desires. Stay close to Me in a simple life of faith and you will be much better off than having many riches and possessions that could distract you from My service. Follow My ways and My plan for your life, and you will find more satisfaction in loving Me and your neighbor."*

Saturday, January 28, 2006: (St. Thomas Aquinas)

At St. John the Evangelist after Communion I could see delicious foods, beautiful homes, and many other gifts all inside a horn of plenty. Jesus said: *"My people, many times you complain about all of the difficult things in life, but you take for granted all of the many gifts that I have provided for you. You have been given jobs to provide for your income so you have enough to eat and pay your bills. In America you have many comforts in your appliances and heating. You have cars for transportation, schools, and good hospitals. Your government does help with money for the poor, the elderly, and some health costs. In the spiritual world you have the gifts of your faith, freedom of religion, and My Most Precious gift of all in Myself present in My Blessed Sacrament.*

With all of these gifts given to you freely, you should be giving Me a prayer of thanksgiving every day. Even your very life, soul, and family are gifts that you sometimes do not every consider. Once you look at all of your blessings, your few little troubles pale in comparison. Sometimes I send you a few trials to keep you humble and test your faith so that you should always be trusting in Me. The fears, that you have, are like the apostles in the boat when a fierce storm overtook them. I rebuked the storm and then I chastised them for such little faith, even when I was with them in person. My people, you also have Me with you, and if a trial should overtake you, you can trust that I will answer your call for help. Certain life events as death and sickness happen, so it cannot always be changed. But you will see ups and downs in your life, and you must be patient to endure the worst and enjoy the good times. Strive to be with Me in all that you do as you love and serve Me. You will see an even greater reward in heaven for being faithful to Me."

Later, at St. Theodore's tabernacle I could see about seven loud speakers at a track for racing horses. The speakers were announcing the beginning of a race. Jesus said: *"My people, this vision was about loudspeakers announcing to the crowd at the race track that the race was about to begin. This represents another calling for several of My messengers to announce that the end times are near. This is also a notice to all of My evangelists that you are in a race against time to save as many souls as possible for the Lord. Some souls may not understand the importance of being saved by Me from hell. Some people are so wrapped up in the world's activities that they never desired to understand My Word in the Scriptures. Some have fallen away from their former faith and are too distracted by the call of worldly things. It is My faithful remnant that I rely on to try and spread My Word to everyone. When the tribulation of the evil ones comes upon you, I have asked you to call on Me and I will have your guardian angels bring you to My refuges of protection. There you will be miraculously protected and provided for. Trust that I will help you in all of your needs, especially in the end days."*

Sunday, January 29, 2006:

At Holy Name after Communion I could see a holy water font at the entrance of a church. Jesus said: *"My people, when you come to church, you make a point to bless yourself with holy water on entering and on leaving. This was part of your early teaching, but it is sometimes more of a response out of habit than really understanding such a blessing. In today's Gospel I rebuked an evil spirit in someone and told the evil spirit to come out quietly. I told you also that I gave this power to expel demons to My apostles and to all of those ordained ministers that are prepared for exorcism. Expelling demons is a battle of spirits and it is better for lay people to pray in groups over a possessed person. This vision of holy water is one of your weapons in praying over someone. Possessed or obsessed people require deliverance prayers of exorcism to call on My Name in expelling the demons to the foot of My cross, so the spirit does not enter anyone else. Exorcist priests should be called on if they are available, but I give this power to My messengers and faithful who take the proper precautions of wearing blessed sacramentals and praying in groups. Pray for people to not be possessed by demons, but be ready to help those in need of spiritual warfare."*

Monday, January 30, 2006:

At Holy Name after Communion I saw a cave or a tomb and there was a device that was spinning very fast. Jesus said: *"My people, Today's Gospel was a special healing of many demons called Legion from a man who lived in the tombs. This is another sign given of such a demon possession where the man had superhuman strength. When I cast this Legion of demons into the swine, there is a mention of two thousand swine. This is another example that people can be possessed by more than one demon, so that exorcisms must take this into account. You can see in this healing that I have more power than many demons combined. You also can see that the demons need to be sent someplace, but preferably to the foot of My cross so they do not enter other persons, animals, or things. This is another example of how I healed the spirit first and then the body. The people were so terrified of the pigs dying and the possessed man healed that they wanted Me to leave their place. This is a hard teaching for people to understand, but it is another emphasis on demon angels that really exist, and how they tempt you and can even possess people if they are invited."*

Later, at St. Theodore's tabernacle I could see an altar of an Indian sacrifice in an old culture. Jesus said: *"My people, you look back at some old civilizations and wonder why they offered up human sacrifices of babies and young women to their gods. Their sacrifices were made on huge altars to gods as the sun and moon. In the Old Testament there is a witness of offering up crops or animals to the One True God. I came as the ultimate Blood Offering to My Father so that all of mankind could be saved from their sins. Even today your culture is different, but you still have gods of comforts, pleasures, money, sports, or possessions. Those things, that you allow to control you or occupy your time before Me, have become your gods. There is only One God and I am the only One worthy of your worship because I created all of you. Today, you make offerings of your babies in abortion up to your gods. With euthanasia you even offer up your older or sick people to put them out of their pain. In the end your people of today are just as callous in their killings, and just as pagan in their worship of gods as these old civilizations. If you truly want to have a respected civilization, then you must stop your abortions and mercy killings, and worship your Lord every day in prayer."*

Tuesday, January 31, 2006: (St. John Bosco)

At Holy Name after Communion I could see a small white balloon travel up into heaven. Jesus said: *"My people, in both of today's readings you have children being grieved by their parents. David grieved for Absolom, his son, and Jairus grieved for his daughter. This is a very difficult time for a parent to have a son or daughter die prematurely. Many parents have had to endure lost children from birth defects or accidents. This rising white balloon in the vision represents the young soul leaving the body. You know that I can call anyone home even in their early years, but man feels more grief when a person dies in their early years. It is easier to accept an older person's death than a young person in man's sense of justice. But each life is a gift and you must be willing to accept My Will even if I should take one of your children before they grow up. In the case of Jairus' daughter, I brought her back from the dead to the pleasure of his family for their faith. Death is a part of life, but man has a difficult time in accepting the finality of losing a loved one. It may be a loss to those still living, but you do not want to deny that person a chance to be in heaven. Children under the age of reason are taken to heaven after their death, so you have saints already in heaven that can be intercessors for your prayer intentions. Souls of people over the age of reason will have to face My judgment at death as even older people do. Pray for those families who suffer the loss of a child because their grieving can disturb them for years if they cannot let them go in their hearts. Only a willing acceptance of My Will can give these parents the peace of mind that they are seeking."*

Later, at St. Theodore's Adoration I could see some high technology vehicles and electronic TVs and computers. Jesus said: *"My people, America still has some advantages in your high technology devices, but your electronic manufacturing is migrating to China, Japan, and Eastern countries of cheap labor. As technology is transferred more overseas, this field could compromise America's leads in the electronic industry. Patents and new inventions are competing for world domination. America's education and know-how need to improve to keep your nation strong in your economy. Many of America's manufacturing jobs are being lost in favor of less paying jobs in the service industries. The American economy is still large, but you are losing market share to foreigners in many fields. America needs to be stronger in your morals, if you are going to maintain your power among the rest of the nations. Love of God and neighbor should be a daily part of your life beyond the striving to be a world leader. Instead of pride and money driving your people, you should put your trust in My help to endure all of your trials. If you desire worldly things more than Me, then you will become a pagan nation destined for destruction."*

Wednesday, February 1, 2006:

At St. John the Evangelist after Communion I could see two fast speed boats ready for take off. Jesus said: *"My people, in the first reading David took a census of his people for adding to his army, and then he repented and had to choose three days of pestilence of his options from the prophet. Many people died from the pestilence as a punishment. The vision shows some readiness for a fast escape, but this is connected with famine and pestilence of the end days which I have warned My faithful to be ready for. A world famine and pestilence will occur after the Warning. This is one of the signs along with a division in My Church, and chips forced in the body that will signal the time to go to My refuges. There will be a moment of haste, so you need to have some things already in your backpacks ready to go. I have asked you to store some blessed sacramentals, holy water, blessed candles, some food to multiply, a few changes of clothes, sleeping bags, a tent, and a small shovel with a bicycle to travel. I will provide for all of your needs at My refuges, as well as protection from the evil ones. Your guardian angels will*

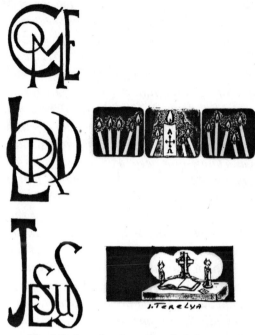

lead you to the nearest refuge. You can look on My luminous crosses to be healed of any diseases that the evil ones will try and inflict on you. See that these things are ready for when you will have to leave in haste."

Later, at St. Theodore's Adoration I could see a lot of electronic gear for reading and detecting microchips. Jesus said: *"My people, your government has passed legislation that is unfunded that will force every state to put a chip in your driver's license that will eventually hold finger prints and iris scans by 2008. Many even admit that this will be a controlled National ID card that will soon be necessary to have to get onto airplanes. It will become a means to buy and sell as you will be tracked by it wherever you go. If your government can mandate chips in your driver's license, they then could mandate these chips in your body so you do not lose them. Refuse to put any chips in your body, even if they threaten to kill you. These chips could have control over your mind. When they mandate chips in the body, then it is time to call on Me and I will have your guardian angels lead you to the nearest refuge of protection. Trust in Me and I will see to your protection and all of your needs will be provided for. These evil ones will try to seek you out in your homes to try and force these chips on you. That is why going to the refuge first would not allow them to find you. If you remain at your homes too long, then they will place you in detention centers to torture and kill you. Trust in My Word to leave your homes before they can find you, and you will be protected from their seeing you."*

Thursday, February 2, 2006: (Presentation of Jesus in the Temple)

At Holy Name after Communion I could see some candles burning and a scene of Jesus being presented as an infant in the temple. Jesus said: *"My people, the vision of the lit candles is a sign that I am the Light that came into this world of darkness of sin. My Light dispels the darkness just as My death on the cross conquered sin and redeemed all of mankind from their sins. The Gospel reading shows the deep faith that Simeon had in believing that he would see his Savior before he died. My Blessed Mother pondered his words about how a sword would pierce her heart in sorrow. Simeon and Anna confirmed to My Blessed Mother and St. Joseph that I am the Savior to come into the world to save My people. Many candles are blessed on this day and they are a representation of My Light that is still in the world. You use candles and My Easter Candle at your Baptism, your marriages, your deaths, and at the Easter Vigil. Even when you will be faced with My three days of darkness at the end of the tribulation, you will need blessed candles for light at that time. Rejoice, as you share the joy of My Light in all of your lives."*

Later, at the prayer group at Holy Name Adoration I could see a crevasse form along an earthquake fault and gradually water fell into the crevasse making it worse. This occurred along the Western coastline of our country. Jesus said: *"My people, an earthquake causes two plates to slip, and when water falls into the crevasse, the earthquake gets worse with more slippage. This can happen along your Western coastline which the fault line follows. I have told you before that you could see some geography change in this area. Many of these events are occurring because of your many sexual sins in this area."*

I could see some men going into a coal mine with a green color around the opening. Jesus said: *"My people, your coal mines are being run to gain the most profit for the owners and the safety of the miners is of less importance to them. Many mines in West Virginia have multiple violations that are not being fixed because of the expense and a threat to the miners' jobs if they tell. Now that these mines have been shut down due to three serious incidents, these violations will need to get fixed before being safe to enter. Greed for profits has put the miners at risk. This is true in other industries where safety is sometimes compromised to cut expenses. Pray for your employers to be more responsible for the safety of their workers."*

I could see a bright light in front of some deer in the north. Jesus said: *"My people, your oil prices have gone up because more countries are using more oil products to run their industries. There is a choice to find more oil in other parts of your country, or truly to focus on using other fuels to be independent of Middle East oil. There have been some improvements in making ethanol, but the amounts sought are so small that it will take decades to replace oil. If oil concerns of the oil companies did not control your economy, you could switch to ethanol in years instead of decades. Pray for your government to do what is best for the people and not what is best for those oil lobbyists controlling alternate fuel production."*

I could see some beautiful buildings where European nations and other countries were debating what to do about Iran making nuclear weapons. Jesus said: *"My people, you have had one threat in North Korea for building nuclear weapons, but they were a threat that could be eased by donations to their poor economy. A similar threat in Iran to build nuclear weapons is different because of their choice to shut down oil production and send oil prices higher. Because Iran does provide oil to Russia and other clients, it will be difficult to have the UN issue any sanctions against Iran. There will be no threat to force Iran to stop making these weapons because even the U.S. cannot extend themselves beyond Iraq. More nuclear weapons in the hands of militant Arabs could cause major instability in the Middle East. Pray for peace in this area that has seen constant wars."*

I could see a smaller volcano sending out dark smoke and ash over a large distance. Jesus said: *"My people, you are seeing several new volcanoes becoming active, especially where you have many earthquakes triggering their eruption. As more volcanoes send more ash into the air, there could be a dramatic effect on your weather. Pray that your weather stabilizes so it does not get too hot or too cold. Otherwise you could see more famines and fires if hotter, or a testing of your fuel supplies if the weather gets colder."*

I could see some demonstrations and riots in the streets as people became upset with their job and finance situations. Jesus said: *"My people, your economists are citing how the average person is spending more than they are earning in salaries. Part of this problem is that families are stressed to find good paying jobs with manufacturing jobs decreasing. Yet housing, fuel costs and education costs are stretching their budgets. This frustration can easily spread to civil unrest in places where business has been poor. Pray for your people to change your government policies, or riots could try to stop the destruction of your middle class."*

I could see an old wood stove being used to heat a house and cook the food. Jesus said: *"My people, as oil and natural gas prices rise and stretch budgets, people may resort to using alternate fuels if they are available and cheap. Some already are using more wood for fires where trees are plentiful and renewable. Many of your choices in how to live are forcing people to change their way of life and what fuels they use. Pray for those who need more money or options of fuel to deal with your high prices."*

Friday, February 3, 2006: (St. Blaise)

At St. John the Evangelist after Communion I could see a rainy day at a funeral and people were looking out of a funeral limousine. Jesus said: *"My people, you are abhorred at the sight of family members killing their spouses and children in the news. Many of these killings come from rage of hate, but the morals of your people are so low and life is not seen as precious anymore to some that even killing could become an option. Already your people's hearts are hardened enough to kill the babies in the womb because your laws allow it. Even the sick and elderly could have their lives taken in euthanasia by sick nurses or doctors, or family seeking inheritances. This extends further to those who think killing in wars is an option if they can make money on other peoples' lives. In poorer neighborhoods drugs are the source of many killings in your cities. If your laws and immorality hold life in such low esteem, then none of your lives are safe, and you are breeding a call for a police state for some kind of order to the killing. Pray for America to change your ways and laws that protect life, or your country will destroy itself."*

Later, at St. Theodore's tabernacle I could see some large, tall antennas for cell phones and microwave signals for radio and television. Even banks and businesses are seen using data signals all over the world with satellites. Jesus said: *"My people, many people think that they have privacy in their lives, but many of your activities are monitored and analyzed everyday. All of your phone calls and e-mails leave a paper trail and are even listened to by your intelligence agencies. All of your charges leave a paper trail and are sold to people that can profile you*

for ads on TV or in the mail. All of your banking is known by govern-
ment agencies, even by your tax bureaus. Your cell phones contain
smart cards that can be tracked anywhere as well as your road debits
for tolls in your smart card passes. To control your buying and selling
by chips in the body is part of what controlling your mind is all about.
The one world people control your lives already with many of your elec-
tronic devices, but do not put chips in your body that could be abused to
control your mind. The time for the Antichrist's declaration is not far
off because these same money people are going to support his control
for their takeover of all countries. The evil ones are duping the rich to
serve them as gods, but I will defeat all of them when I come again to
renew the earth of all evil. Trust in Me and My power instead of the
control of the demons and the rich people."

Saturday, February 4, 2006: (John Paul Lyons' funeral, 20 months)
At Holy Spirit after Communion I could see people of varying ages
approaching an escalator going up. There was also an opposite sign of
souls going down to earth into the newly conceived children. Jesus said:
"My people, this scene of people of various ages waiting to go up an
escalator represents the souls that I take home in death. The other vi-
sion is of souls coming down to earth as each child is conceived. There
are souls constantly coming and going in the repeating cycle of life.
It is unfortunate in your eyes when a life is cut short and the grieving
process begins. But in respect to eternal life, all life on earth is short.
That is why each day is a blessed opportunity to love Me and each
other in helping one another. You are mourning for the lost little one,
but you still have comfort from your living family members as you are
blessed with a new saint in heaven. Your life's mission goes on and you
are called to continue your own path until you also are ready to come
home with Me. You heard in the Gospel how I want you to be faithful
as a little child's faith of humility and innocence. Life is very precious
and it needs to be nurtured and protected, just as your faith in Me."
Later, at St. Theodore's tabernacle I could see a clock in the dirt that was
very close to twelve o'clock. Jesus said: *"My people, in the days of your*
cold war when it was possible for a nuclear exchange, you represented
this situation by moving the hands of a clock closer to twelve o'clock. I
am showing you this clock again in the vision because Iran and North
Korea are getting close to having their own nuclear bombs. When the

Iranian President threatened to attack the U.S. and Israel, he was showing what he would do with such nuclear devices. If he wanted to ruin the American economy, he could use three EMP (Electromagnetic pulse) *devices over New York, Washington, and Silicon Valley to eliminate all microchips in those areas. These devices would throw your banking system into chaos until other chips could be made to replace them. Your technology is very fragile and needs to be protected or backed up with older technology. If Arab militants had access to nuclear devices, there could be some serious consequences if they used them. You have seen how destructive they can be with conventional explosives, so imagine how dangerous they could be with weapons of mass destruction. Such oil countries could then use oil and nuclear weapons as blackmail for their demands. Once one country would set off these weapons, this could trigger multiple responses that could endanger the health of all of mankind. Pray again that wars as this will be prevented, and logical thinking will prevail over using nuclear bombs.*"

Sunday, February 5, 2006:

At Holy Name after Communion I could see two tablets representing the Ten Commandments and a large water well representing Jacob's Well. Jesus said: *"My people, the Old Testament is steeped in tradition as My Church was rooted in the Law which I came to fulfill. There are traditions in My Church as well, but they serve to support My Word in the Gospel and give the faithful an example to follow in their faith. You have traditional prayers as the rosary which is a remembrance of the 150 psalms and the various important steps in My life portrayed in the Mysteries. You have My Mass and receive Holy Communion on Sunday to share your faith with others and fulfill your obligation to worship on Sunday. You have My hierarchy in the pope, cardinals, bishops, and priests that carry out My ministry. You have My Commandments to follow and can be healed of your sins in Confession. You have My sacraments and My Liturgy of the Hours for daily prayer. Most of all I draw you to love Me and your neighbors in faith. When people fall away from their faith, it is a testimony that their faith was not nurtured or that their roots were weak without proper teaching or encouragement. Love takes a commitment to practice what you believe and preach. If your faith is not an integral part of your life, then it will soon die of your lack of love and interest. That is why daily prayer is an important part of your life*

as well as following My traditions which are there to support your faith. Believe that I am your Savior who awaits you in heaven, and show your belief by loving Me and loving your neighbor."

Monday, February 6, 2006: (St. Paul Miki and companions)

At Holy Name after Communion I could see a dark box that held the Ten Commandments in the Ark of the Covenant. Then I saw a tomb with gold sparkles glowing all around it and in the air. This was where Jesus resurrected. Jesus said: *"My people, the Ten Commandments given to Moses on the two tablets of stone was the covenant between God and the Jewish people. There truly was the presence of God in the cloud around these tablets. The vision of My tomb and My Resurrection is another covenant of even more significance. My death on the cross was the ultimate sacrifice that you renew at every Mass, and you are redeemed from your sins. This example of My Resurrection is a foreshadowing of all of My faithful souls that one day they will also be resurrected with their bodies. There is a new covenant and My Real Presence is now in every consecrated Host in every tabernacle where My Blessed Sacrament resides. When you want to pray to Me or give Me praise and worship, you can visit Me in My tabernacle, Adoration, or receive Me in Holy Communion. My holy Presence at your local church awaits your presence to share My love with you. Give praise and glory to God for My gift of Myself to you in My Eucharist."*

Later, at St. Theodore's tabernacle I could see a wall and then a scene of a wheel with many cogs. Jesus said: *"My people, this picture of a wheel represents man's vision of the wheels of progress. You have seen many new inventions and electricity has provided the power for your many electrical devices. Some of these inventions save you time, but they also have side effects that man has traded off for what he wants. Your cars give you travel, but you pay in pollution and for your dependence on oil. You have medicines to stop diseases and you are living longer, but some side effects can ruin your internal organs. You have increased the harvest of your crops by using artificial fertilizers, and manipulated DNA for your crops to endure bugs and bad weather. Much of your pollution and changes in your food are causing an increase in cancer and other diseases. Man wants progress on his terms and in his time without concerning himself with how he is upsetting the balance of nature. This is why you are seeing unusual storms and unusual seasons as the hot and cold of your winter. When I return, I will renew the earth to its time before man has destroyed My plan of perfection. Then you will see a new heavens and a new earth in My Era of Peace."*

Tuesday, February 7, 2006:

At St. John the Evangelist after Communion I could see a door opening and I was low, looking from the bottom of the door. Jesus said: *"My people, today's Gospel is asking you to open the door to your spiritual life to let some fresh air come into your stale air of complacency and feeling that you deserve everything. Being low at the door means that you should practice more humility in your actions, instead of ordering everyone around according to your desires. You need to respect everyone's right to their own opinion and likes. You all are different and you need to have compromise in living peacefully with others. You have many earthly customs and traditions, but your first priority should be to love God and to love your neighbor. You can encourage others to love Me and their neighbors, but do not try to force religion on others because it must come from their own free will and not yours. I love everyone and I want all of you to follow My Commandments on your path to heaven, but I do not force My love on anyone. True love has to come from the hearts of both parties freely. You can give good example and a gracious nudging to Mass and Confession, but do not nag your children on every little custom. By your prayers and teaching, I will open their hearts to My love, but each person has to make their own personal decision to love Me and their neighbor."*

Later, at St. Theodore's Adoration I could see several baskets of food left over. Jesus said: *"My people, the baskets full of left over food refers to My two miracles where I multiplied the food for the five thousand and the four thousand. The number seven and twelve are all throughout these accounts. With the five thousand there were five loaves of bread and two*

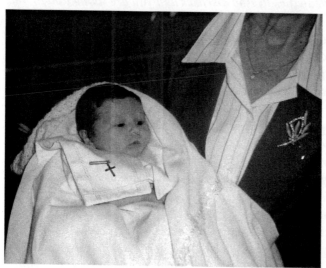

fish adding up to seven. After the people ate their fill, twelve baskets of food were collected from the left overs. With the four thousand there were seven loaves to start and after the people ate, there were seven baskets of left overs collected. These miracles showed My power, but also it was respectful of not wasting the food left over. These baskets also show you that I will give you My gifts that will more than satisfy your needs. These miracles of the bread being multiplied also can be seen in how the Bread of Holy Communion is also multiplied, yet I am fully present in each Host. This is also a forerunner for how I will multiply the food for My faithful in the tribulation time. For those without a Mass, I will have My angels bring you Communion so I can be with you all days, even up to when I return."

Wednesday, February 8, 2006:

At St. John the Evangelist after Communion I could see snow coming down on a winter day. Jesus said: *"My people, each day of your life*

*brings you one step closer to Me in your judgment. I want My faithful
to live humble, simple, and holy lives, and you will be worthy of coming
to heaven. Today's Gospel speaks of what comes from the heart is what
defiles a man and not just what he eats. Even though you may wash your
hands and perform outward acts that appear proper, it is your thoughts
that direct your actions. I look into the intention of your actions, so
you are not fooling Me in what you are really thinking. Focus your
lives on Me and serve Me, and you will have nothing to fear. I take
care of My own in miraculous ways as I help provide for all of your
family's needs. Do not be like the worldly who ask what are we to eat,
drink, and what clothes are we to wear. If you seek first the kingdom
of God, all of these things will be granted to you. Your mission is to
know, love, and serve Me, as well as evangelize souls to be with Me in
heaven. Trust in Me and I will answer your prayer intentions."*

Later, at St. Theodore's tabernacle I could see a picture frame window
of a store with all of their items for sale, but in the middle of the scene there
was a black shadow. It looked like someone with macular degeneration.
Jesus said: *"My people, you have read of Me healing blind people so they
could see again physically. There are also spiritually blind people that
need to be enlightened by My grace. This vision of a black shadow in
the middle of a scene represents how evil influences can take over your
thoughts and control your life. Distractions by possessions and desires
of worldly pleasures can take you away from your focus on Me. You
need to hang on to your daily prayers and daily Mass for the strength
that you need to keep Me first in your life. Do not let your spiritual
blindness increase, but come to Me in Confession so I can let you fully
see by My grace, so earthly things will not disturb you. You notice the
symptoms of physical blindness and you go to the doctor. Look also
for signs of your spiritual blindness and come to your greatest Healer
in Me."*

Thursday, February 9, 2006:

At St. John the Evangelist after Communion I could see a large crucifix over the globe of the earth. Jesus said: *"My people, this vision of
My crucifix over the globe of the earth means that I died on the cross
for all peoples of the earth and not just for the Promised People of
Israel. Unless everyone worships God and obeys My Commandments,
they cannot enter heaven. I have sent My apostles, deacons, and mis-*

sionaries as St. Paul to all parts of the world so My message of love is available to everyone. You cannot have strange gods before Me as idols because this is against My First Commandment. If you put other beliefs, possessions, fame, or riches as idols before Me, then you will be like the lukewarm that I condemned because they speak of Me with their lips, but their hearts are far from Me. A time of the Warning will come upon you when you will be drawn out of your body before Me and I will reveal Myself as the Son of God to each person. I will show everyone that belief in My Catholic Church, that I established on earth, holds the most complete knowledge of My Revelation which is complete with My sacraments. Everyone will have their lives shown to them of their good and bad actions, and the guilt of your sins will be a call for repentance and a seeking of forgiveness. You will be placed back into your bodies for an opportunity to change your lives of sin and follow Me in obeying My Commandments of love. If you refuse to worship God and you disobey My laws without repentance, then you are on the road to hell."

Later, at the prayer group at Holy Name Adoration I could see a crucifix on a pole being carried in the streets among some crowds. Jesus said: *"My people, the latest militant protests against some cartoons demeaning Muhammad in European newspapers is causing a burning of embassies. It has been revealed that an Iranian even added to the protests by faking further worse cartoons and claimed it was from European sources. You are seeing many trumped up reasons to cause hate between Muslims and other peoples. Recently, My Crucifixion has been mocked and there are hardly any complaints, but it was removed. Catholic Doctrine is made fun of because there is not much defense made. Pray for all of these evil doers who will have to make an accounting before Me for their bad actions."*

I could see fires in some places and snow in others. Jesus said: *"My people, your weather and natural disasters are continuing even during the winter months. Your scientists have declared a new record for a high average temperature in January. While some are getting snow and usual cold temperatures now, others in Florida, Texas, and California have such low humidity that fires are ravaging these states. Many new records are being set every year so that you are seeing continual signs of the coming end days. Pray and prepare for your spiritual deliverance through the coming tribulation."*

I could see an oil rigging that was producing more oil. Jesus said: *"My people, your oil prices and commodities have been going up and down when there are threats to your oil supplies or a threat to interest rate changes. Even your houses and car sales have affected your stock prices. Many budget calls and deficits are going to affect various groups where cuts are being made to pay for more of your billions spent on the Iraq War. Continuous wars against terrorists are manufactured and your people are asking for more answers than they are being given. Continue to pray for the end of this Iraq War before your casualties and money spent get out of control."*

I could see some large white spheres that were intelligence equipment listening to all communications. Jesus said: *"My people, your government is claiming that they have the right to intercept foreign calls to militant groups without answering to anyone for a warrant. The truth is that this is just a cover-up because they are listening to all sources of communication and they do not want to admit this to the public. Better to talk quietly outside because your conversations are being monitored on your phone lines and through your TVs. Do not be afraid because I will protect you at My refuges."*

I could see many people watching sports games on TV. Jesus said: *"My people, there are some people who spend many hours watching sports events that could easily become addicting. However you spend your time, you need to be careful not to let anything control your mind and body away from Me and your prayer time. If you spend most of your free time on selfish entertainment, then you need to reset your priorities so you can give Me more love and time to serve Me. By constantly analyzing how you spend your time, then you can see if you are letting things control you."*

I could see people buying blessed sacramentals to protect themselves and others from evil influences. Jesus said: *"My people, I am happy to see that you are finally taking some actions to prepare yourselves for the coming tribulation. There will be many demons released from hell at that time and My faithful will need all of the spiritual weapons that you can muster for this battle of good and evil. Trust in Me that I will protect you from the evil ones at My refuges, and My martyrs will receive My grace to endure their pain at that time."*

I could see some people in the stores buying gifts for Valentine's Day. Jesus said: *"My people, many spouses and sweethearts are making their plans to share with each other their love on St. Valentine's Day. This is a nice gesture once a year, but there should be a constant celebration of love with Me and your neighbor all year long. I have asked you to love everyone, even your enemies or those that you avoid seeing. Try to make more of an attempt to reach out and show your care for all the people that come into your life with a special emphasis on doing this out of love for Me."*

Friday, February 10, 2006: (St. Scholastica)

At St. John the Evangelist after Communion I could see piles of palm for Lent and the purple covered statues. Then I saw the somber life of a monastery. Jesus said: *"My people, daily prayer should be an important part of your spiritual life. There were several saints that led monastic lives of prayer and started various orders of priests and nuns. The practice of the Liturgy of the Hours can be prayed at various times of the day and night. In the Gospels it is recorded several times how I went to the mountains to pray and prepare Myself spiritually for events that I was about to face. This is a good preparation for when you have hard things to accomplish either physically or spiri-*

tually. Prayer in the morning helps ready you for the day's events, and prayer at night is a thanksgiving for My help and a time to ponder any mistakes so you can improve your life. You have My strength in prayer because you are being united with Me in your expression of love for Me. Even at times it is good to be open to listening to My directions and discernment for what you are to do in life. Keep your focus on My mission for you, and you will be on the narrow road to heaven."

Later, at St. Theodore's tabernacle I could see some row houses and a very cold winter in Europe. Jesus said: *"My people, this view of a severe winter cold in Europe is in stark contrast to the warmest January on record in your country. Your scientists are baffled on how you can have such extreme hot and cold in the same Northern Hemisphere when it should be winter. Other scientists speak of changing jet streams which have for a while been staying North allowing in the warm air. It is no surprise that your HAARP machine has been active and it could cause the jet streams to stay in one position longer than normal. Man has been experimenting with microwave weather making machines for some time. Much of your pollution, wars, and changing of your food is contributing to an upset in the balance of nature. Man thinks that he can change things to improve on My perfection in creation. All of your activities are threatening your very survival because of the abuse of your weapons. Pray that My hand will hold back your nuclear bombs from destroying everyone. I will not let you or the devil destroy all of My creation. Pray and thank Me that you are secure in My help without worry of what will happen during the tribulation."*

Saturday, February 11, 2006: (Our Lady of Lourdes)

At St. John the Evangelist after Communion I could see some gold ore and rays of light were shining off the rocks. Jesus said: *"My people, in the desert while Moses was receiving the Ten Commandments, My promised people made a golden calf to worship, even though they had just witnessed My saving power from the Egyptians. Worshiping this idol of gold may seem unusual to your modern day habits, but they were imitating the worship of false gods as their neighboring nations did. I made many covenants with My promised people and there was a division in the camp on who should follow My Law with Moses, and who would continue to worship other gods and idols. Even in today's world you see times of gold rushes in California and now a rush to gambling casinos and lotteries with a desire to get rich quick. Man still is challenged to worship gods in possessions, money, and fame. Some people spend their whole lives working as much as possible to accumulate great wealth and then it is gone in a few seconds when they die. I have given you a message about seeking riches:* (Matt. 6:19-21) 'Do not lay up for yourselves treasures on earth, where rust and moth consume, and where thieves break in and steal; but lay up for yourselves treasures in heaven, where neither rust nor moth consumes, nor thieves break in and steal. For where thy treasures are, there also will thy heart be. You cannot serve God and worldly goods.' *You will either love Me, the real Treasure, or you will love your worldly things, but you cannot have two masters. Where you spend your time and what you desire in your heart will determine if you choose Me over your wealth."*

Sunday, February 12, 2006:

At Holy Name after Communion I could see a grotto where people prayed. Then I saw a view of heaven above with each saint holding a candle meaning that they had been purified. Then I saw some soul bodies burning in the flames of purgatory and hell. Jesus said: *"My people, you all have to realize that you are all sinners and need to be healed of your own spiritual leprosy. I have given you My sacrament of Reconciliation so you can be changed from unclean to a clean, pure soul full of grace. So many souls are quick to point out other people's sins and any unusual physical appearance, but they need to cleanse their own sinful appearance to Me. You are seeing a vision of the saints in heaven after their purification either on earth or in purgatory. Better to cleanse the punishment due to your sins here on earth than later in purgatory where the suffering is more difficult. In purgatory you will see flames of purgation in the lower levels as well as the pain of not seeing Me until you are released. Remember also to pray for your soul and the souls suffering in purgatory who can be released sooner with your prayers."*

Later, at St. Theodore's tabernacle I could see a large view of a dark sports stadium. Jesus said: *"My people, this scene of a dark stadium is a reflection on the words that I gave you of how the Antichrist represents the darkness of evil that will try and lead souls to worship him only. Stadiums can hold large crowds and the Antichrist will have a charisma to draw people to follow him for power and gain. There is a progression of how the Antichrist will come to power. Unless I give the word, he cannot declare himself ruler of this world. In many churches there are statues, icons, and large crucifixes being removed and the tabernacles put in back rooms. This is in preparation to bring in idols of the New Age and the occult. New Age teachings and exercises will be gradually brought into My churches. As the Antichrist gains more power, you will even see the image of the beast being placed on My altars. As soon as you see New Age idols and teachings brought into a church, leave that church for an underground faithful remnant church that is true to My teachings. Avoid looking at or listening to the Antichrist because his demonic powers of suggestion could lead you to worship him. Hold on to your faith and traditions about Me, and you will have no worries. Trust in My protection both now and at My refuges."*

Monday, February 13, 2006:

At St. John the Evangelist after Communion I could see underwater and a large bunch of bubbles were released when an earthquake occurred, induced by the HAARP machine. Jesus said: *"My people, you have seen in your news and I have confirmed that your HAARP machine, sponsored by your government, can cause earthquakes and weather making. By controlling the jet streams around strong storms, this microwave machine can worsen hurricanes and now your snow storms. This machine sends out constant broadcasts of high intensity microwave bursts from many acres of antennae so that it warms the ionosphere and controls how long a jet stream will stay in place. The vision shows a disturbance of an earthquake underwater that can also be induced by disturbing the magnetic makeup of the earth's crust. This manipulation of nature and the earth by your electronic devices is another way that man is upsetting the rain and snowfall that could cause more fires and famines throughout the world. When I send you natural disasters because of your sins, it is also a punishment for all of your mischief that is affecting the earth's weather. When I come again, I will cleanse the earth of all of your evil people, and restore the earth to its original balance that man has distorted."*

Later, at Our Lady of Lourdes Adoration I could see a table and an ugly demon lay in wait to tempt someone that would come to that table. Jesus said: *"My people, you are constantly beset by demons in their temptations every day. They use your pride and your earthly desires to distract you from your prayers and Me by wasting your time on frivolous earthly things. You love to lavish yourself with earthly entertainment in movies, news, TV shows, or curious shopping. Some spend too much time in casinos, on the internet, or on other hobbies that do nothing to serve Me. You should have your prayer time focused on Me as your first priority, and put aside all of your addictions, and avoid near occasions of sin for your habitual sin. If you focus on actions that are good and serve Me in love for your neighbor, then you will have less time to be drawn into your earthly distractions and sins. As you see this vision of the demons waiting to lure you into their temptations, call on My Name to take away these temptations, and do not entertain them that lead you into sin. When you are more conscious of the demon attacks every day, then you will be able to strengthen yourself against sin. I am with you every day and I wait for you to call on My help, and for you to show your love for Me."*

Tuesday, February 14, 2006: (St. Cyril, St. Methodius, St. Valentine)
At St. Charles after Communion I could see a sculpture that someone had made by hand. Jesus said: *"My people, you all have been endowed with a unique set of talents and skills as this sculptor in the vision. There is a source, or cause of these gifts that you have, and it is Me, your Creator. Along with your skills, you have also been blessed with a mission in how best to use your talents for My greater glory. I do not want My people to bury your talents, or refuse to use them because you were meant to carry out your mission that only you were directed to follow. On this day people are thinking of human love between a man and a woman, but you can think of loving Me every day and thanking Me for My gifts. If you follow My Commandments, it also means that you should love all of your neighbors as well. As in other languages there are various forms of love. The agape love is man's love for his God, and the filial love is your love for one and other. The Eros love, or earthly love is only intended for those that are married. You can direct your actions to do everything out of love for Me so that you are desiring to follow My Will rather than your own. When you live a life of service, you will not have time to be selfish. Love has to be shown both to Me and your spouse, so do not be afraid to love Me in prayer and do good things for your spouse."*

Later, at St. Theodore's Adoration I could see an airport and there were loudspeakers broadcasting information about everyone that was flying. Jesus said: *"My people, over the next few years your government will demand that you have a driver's license that contains all of your personal information with fingerprints embedded in a smart card. The loudspeakers at the airport represent how they would be broadcasting all of your information so crooks could use this to get into your bank accounts and steal your money with a false identity theft. It will be mandatory to have such a smart card license or you will not be able to get onto an airplane. All of this is being required because of your desire for security, even at the cost of your freedoms. The Arab attackers that crashed the planes into the trade towers had fake documents to get their driver's licenses. These smart cards could also be manipulated with fake Ids, and the only people monitored, will be your law abiding citizens. See that terrorism and these attacks were all staged purposely to give authority to your government to control its citizens. When these chips are demanded next into your bodies, then you will have to call on Me, and My angels will lead you to safety at My refuges. Have no fear because My power is greater than all the demons and evil people."*

Wednesday, February 15, 2006:

At St. John the Evangelist after Communion I could see someone crouching behind some chairs in secret trying to avoid being seen. Jesus said: *"My people, in today's Gospel I healed a man from blindness so that he could see, and because of his faith in My healing. There are other kinds of blindness to sin when people try to cheat others out of what is theirs. Some employers are cheating their employees by cutting their benefits, not paying a living wage, and diminishing or eliminating their pensions. Some governments levy too high a tax unfairly on unsuspecting home owners. Some taxpayers cheat on their taxes by not claiming their correct income or deductions. Some businesses do not report all of their income or make purposeful errors in predicting their income. These same businesses also avoid taxes offshore or send their jobs abroad to get cheaper labor. All of these things are slights of hand in secret to steal or embezzle money at other people's expense. This blindness to fairness and cheating is done on purpose to gain riches improperly and even unlawfully. Pray for these people to change their ways and that they may be brought to justice. If they are not chastised here on earth, they will be punished at their judgment before Me."*

Later, at St. Theodore's Adoration I could see some very rustic pottery to carry water and then I could see some canned food in a storage pantry. Jesus said: *"My people, I have warned you to prepare yourselves for a time of persecution and tribulation when the evil ones will be allowed a brief reign on this earth. It is not an easy thought to contemplate leaving your house and all of your possessions behind. But the chaos will be great and you may be faced with either martyrdom for your faith or following My angels to refuges. The refuges, that will be protected, will be rustic as in the vision, and you may have crude utensils to eat and drink with. You will see miraculous springs at My refuges that will provide water for many people. The canned food that I asked people to store is seen in the vision that will be multiplied for your food. I keep telling My faithful not to worry about what you are to eat and drink, or what you are to wear. Just as I take care of you now, so I will protect you from the evil one at My refuges. Trust in My constant multiplication of all that you need, and you will see how generous I am with all of My gifts for you. You will always be given enough grace to endure all the trials that you will face. So have no fear and thank Me for watching over all of you."*

Thursday, February 16, 2006:

At St. John the Evangelist after Communion I could see people gathered together at Mass. Jesus said: *"My people, in today's Gospel I asked My disciples: 'Who do you say that I am?' After they had seen My miracles and listened to My words in explaining My parables, My apostles still did not always know Me and My purpose, since they were not yet enlightened by the Holy Spirit. But St. Peter was inspired to say: 'Thou art the Christ, the Son of the Living God.' It is one thing to see and hear what I did and said, but it is another to live My words and act on them. The Jewish people are My Promised people, and they were waiting for the Messiah, but most of them did not recognize Me as their Savior. Those, who are faithful to My words and act on them, are called My Elect on their path to heaven. But I ask My faithful also to listen to these words and ask yourself if you really believe that I am your Savior who came to die for your sins. Once you say that you believe, then you must accept Me as your Creator, Savior, and Healer. Now you have a responsibility to love Me and your neighbor as yourself. You need to follow My Will and My mission for your life. Faith in Me is a life long commit-*

ment to respond to following My Commandments and strive for that perfection in your life that will lead you to heaven. Give Me praise and glory as you worship Me and imitate My life of holiness. I have given you My sacrament of Reconciliation so you can have your sins forgiven frequently and keep a pure soul. I have given you a gift of My Real Presence every time that you receive Me in

Holy Communion and visit Me in Adoration or at My tabernacle. If you are called to be My Elect, then you must not be lazy in the ways of the world, but you must show your love for Me and evangelize as many souls as you can to be saved in My grace."

Later, at the prayer group at Holy Name Adoration I could see a beautiful Persian Rug and there was a mirror reflecting what it looked like. Jesus said: *"My people, many times you do not realize how much you crave earthly things until you look in the mirror to see your own actions. It is your thoughts that are behind your actions, and you need to step back quietly and review how much you do for Me and how much you do for yourself. If you are desiring to be holy, then you must detach yourself more from earthly things. All that you do for Me and your neighbor will gain you more riches in heaven than all the wealth of this world that you accumulate."*

I could see a dark root cellar where people have stored some extra food for the tribulation. Jesus said: *"My people, there are some people with some money that have heard a call to start a refuge. Looking to establish a refuge should come only after strong prayer and discernment. The land of a refuge should be consecrated to Me and there usually are springs of water on this land. Some have built some structures on the land with some animals and have stored food and blankets. I will bless all of My faithful who have been called to start a refuge. During the tribulation these places will be protected havens for My faithful."*

I could see some fins on a heating device that could be used during power outages. Jesus said: *"My people, I have warned you to have some backup fuel supplies in case you have power outages or a shortage of fuel. Many disasters could occur that could shut down your power lines or gas lines. Many current riots for various reasons could close down oil pipelines or threaten to restrict your gasoline supplies. Pray for My help to keep peace in your world."*

I could see both plants and animals give glory to God in their very existence. Jesus said: *"My people, I call your attention to the order and beauty on the earth when you study the plants and animals before man has changed them by hybrids and breeding. I created this order and balance of nature as it was perfectly made. Even looking at mankind's physical makeup will show you miracles in how wonderfully you are made. Man in his quest for better crops has changed the seeds for various purposes. He has bred animals for meat, but you also have added drugs and feed to fatten them quicker. Man needs to protect his environment by not changing My original plan."*

I could see some centers to handle flood and hurricane victims. Jesus said: *"My people, in previous years you have had good weather without so many disastrous events. Recently, your large cities have had to deal with major fires and hurricanes that you were not prepared to handle. Pray for these people that were ravaged by storms and still are struggling to find proper lodging. Put yourself in their shoes without much money and you will understand their pain."*

I could see some large waves and disasters from unusual storms. Jesus said: *"My people, your storms and disasters are entering into a warmer period that will only make them grow worse and more frequent. Your only protection will be to move away from rivers, lakes, and the oceans. Weather patterns are changing more and they are setting new records every year. I will protect you from this violence, but the violence of man is spreading all over the world in many killings. Stop your wars and the killing of innocent people as in abortions. Pray for people to use the natural order of things and refrain from cloning and other abuses of manipulating DNA.”*

I could see man's work to improve things in the use of science, but more money is wasted on wars and developing weapons instead of helping the poor and the hungry. Jesus said: *“My people, there are many people who go to bed hungry every day, yet man spends money on frivolous things as wars and weapons. Your country is one of the largest arms makers in the world and your deficits from war and free trade are going to cause your bankruptcy and takeover by foreign countries. Your central bankers are looking for wars to make money on the arms and the interest on your debts. Unless your people take back control over your decisions for war and overspending your budgets, everyone will be sharing in the grand bankruptcy that will allow your country to be taken over by foreigners. Pray to improve your morals and repent of your sins, or worse things will befall you.”*

Friday, February 17, 2006:

At St. John the Evangelist after Communion I could see a large oil tanker in the water steaming right toward Me. Jesus said: *“My people, at one time America used to consume almost forty percent of the world's available energy supplies and yet you have only five percent of the world's population. Now you are using only twenty-five percent of the world's fuels because China and other industrial countries are competing more for America's standard of living in manufacturing. The demands for oil, natural gas, and other fuels are soon going beyond the abilities to produce these fuels. I am showing this oil tanker in the vision because the sources of oil are in many political hot spots that could easily upset America's oil supplies. As your deficits with other nations go higher, it will be beneficial to your nation to start using more renewable sources of energy than depending on foreign oil. Your government deficits with overspending and your trade deficits are out of control, and they are eroding the strength of your economy. America needs to keep its industries at home so you are not dependent on buy-*

ing things from countries like China. Soon and even presently your largest exports will only be agricultural products. Stripping America of its factories and economic strength is a part of the one world people's strategy for taking over your nation when it goes into bankruptcy. This exporting of jobs and money through wars and trade is a part of this planned takeover. As long as the American people allow your government to get into costly wars, and control your jobs and spending, your fate will be sealed. Your people also need to repent of their sexual sins and abortions, or you will see more destruction from natural disasters. Change your ways before others will take you over."

Later, at St. Theodore's tabernacle I could see a wheel with spokes for steering a ship, but it was running loose without any control at the helm. Jesus said: *"My people, this vision of a ship without any direction represents America's leadership problem today. Your Congress and President are being controlled by the one world people in the central bankers. It appears that they are not protecting the people's interest, but they are following a course of destruction which is how the one world people will take over. These mistakes in more wars and free trade that ships your jobs overseas are not just by accident, but it is a plan to destroy your country so the Antichrist and evil people can come to power. It is obvious to everyone that your budget deficits are out of control because of the billions of dollars being spent on your Iraq war. You are becoming dependent on foreign countries for fuel and all manufactured goods, and this is another disaster to your jobs and your economy. Your country is also without direction when it comes to your morality as well. Your sexual sins and abortions continue on with no remorse or repentance. Many of your sins are causing your own punishment in your mistakes and natural disasters. As you turn your back to Me, you are refusing My blessings and graces that have made your country strong. The American people need to repent of their sins, and take back control of your country from the rich, or you will continue on your road to destruction without any proper direction."*

Saturday, February 18, 2006:

At St. John the Evangelist after Communion I could see a bulging granary and then a very small spigot to feed the people. Jesus said: *"My people, wars and insurrections have caused famines and have destroyed economies all over the world. There are many poor and hungry people that are not receiving any aid. America contributes food and aid to some countries, but the amount of money spent on foreign wars dwarfs any amount spent on aid. You are the widow's mite handing out aid, but you are an uncontrolled spender when it comes to wars and weapons. I keep telling you, if there were no wars, your defense industrial complex would have no reason to exist except for home defense. The one world people need to generate reasons for war to justify your government's reckless spending. These people continue to profit from your war debts in interest which the taxpayer gives them, and they make money on the arms' sales. You can see the double standard where you are fighting in Iraq because of nuclear weapon fears, but you are doing nothing physical against Iran and North Korea who are obviously building nuclear weapons. War and killing are the tools of the demons, so how long is America going to continue this carnage of lives and spending which is not changing anything in these countries? Pray for an end of these wars and concentrate more on being peacemakers than war makers."*

Sunday, February 19, 2006:

At Holy Name after Communion I could see a mat being carried down some winding stairs and then a view opened up to a banquet table set for a large meal. Jesus said: *"My people, in today's Gospel you can identify with the brokenness of the paralytic man. Life makes many demands of you in schooling, making a living at work, and caring for your family. During the stress of all that you go through, there is a certain brokenness of your trials in everyone's life. You all have health problems, or you are helping someone with health problems. Going down the stairs in the vision represents all that you go through in life. But then I am there to tell everyone: 'Your sins are forgiven.' I do not force you to come to Me, but those, who seek Me in repentance and sorrow for their sins, receive My forgiveness and grace of a pure soul. When you see this banquet table in the vision, this represents the reward awaiting My faithful in heaven for all those struggling through life. When you call on Me for help, I am at your side to lessen your burden and give you the grace to endure anything that you may face on earth. It is reassuring to know that I always love you, and you always have a friend in Me to listen to your troubles and petitions. Your love for Me will be multiplied many times over in My gifts to you. Repent of your sins and love Me, and you will see your reward both here and in heaven."*

Later, at St. Theodore's tabernacle I could see a new scientific device circling very fast and then a light beam transported something to another place. Jesus said: *"My people, your scientists in different countries have worked on many different kinds of light beams for weapons to kill people. It is very difficult and time consuming to send troops, tanks, and ships to far away places. That is why your military desires a non-destructive light beam that could transport large objects from one place to another in a very short time. There are some early signs that this can be done, but it is being guarded with high security as the next phase of stealth technology. Already the Russians are using special beam weapons for killing that disintegrate bodies leaving them irradiated, but not by nuclear radiation. All the billions of dollars spent on your military are to develop the next generation of weapons that are sophisticated in their design and expensive to make. This money could be better put to use in feeding the poor of the world."*

Monday, February 20, 2006:

At Holy Name after Communion I could see a dark room with a large trash bin full of bags of garbage. Jesus said: *"My people, at times your waste baskets get full, or you are cleaning out your basement. Then you dispose of your waste into a large receptacle for the garbage man. In the spiritual world your souls collect a lot of garbage in your sins and you need to dump them also. I am your spiritual garbage man who cleanses your sins and takes them away, but My priest sons assist Me when you come to Me in them for Confession. But there must be enough faith in each person to desire forgiveness and to make the forward motion to come to Confession. The father in the Gospel wanted his son healed of his demon possession, but his faith in Me to heal his son was weak. That is why he asked Me to help his unbelief. Faith is a gift, but it must be nourished by prayer in calling on My help to endure life. When My apostles could not cause the demon to leave the boy, I sighed in wondering how long will My apostles also be weak in the use of their gifts. I told them that some demons were harder to cast out, and this type required sustained prayer and fasting. (Mark 9:28) When you pray as a group in My Name, you can cast out demons with prayer and fasting, but you need to be more persistent with some demons than others. This little prayer of the father could be your prayer also when he said: 'I do believe, help my unbelief.'"* (Mark 9:23)

Later, at St. Theodore's tabernacle I could see two reels of tape being played back that represented a playback in time of our lives as in the Warning or at death. Jesus said: *"My people, these reels of tape being rewound and played back in the vision represents how I will review your life outside of*

time at the coming Warning and at your death or near death experiences. You will fast speed through your sleeping hours, but all of your thoughts and conversations will be reviewed. Sometimes the evil one takes advantage of your bad memories to taunt you, but when you call on My Name, I will take away any stressful temptations. Many times you do not realize how much you offended Me in your bad actions. You also will see your sins of omission when you could have done some good deeds and you refused. It is better even if you balk at a good deed and finally do it, than to say you will, and later refuse to do it. (Matt 21:28-32) *I do not force you to do good deeds out of love, but I want you to choose on your own to help people. It is this free will choice that I give everyone, but you all will be held accountable for what you did with all of your opportunities. In the Warning and near death experiences you will be brought back into your bodies to change your bad habits and live holier lives. But at death there will be no changing of your judgment. Now is the time to make some changes in your life so you can start working toward your crown of sainthood. The more you allow your sins to hold you captive in your earthly desires, the harder it will be to confess your sins to Me in the priest. I want each of you to spiritually let go of all of the entanglements that keep you from loving Me. Be free to open your heart and soul to Me and you will find true happiness in even carrying your daily cross. Love Me and your neighbor as yourself and this will be your life long work to save your soul."*

Tuesday, February 21, 2006: (St. Peter Damian)

At Holy Name after Communion I could see a tomb of a saint and a small statue appeared as a holographic three-dimensional image over the tomb. Jesus said: *"My people, you should revere My saints more since they are models of behavior for you to imitate. Some people have statues, icons, and relics of the saints to commemorate their lives, and they are great intercessors for prayers. To be saints they usually have several miracles associated with their intercession. You have various favorite saints to pray to and still miracles are resulting. To live like a saint means that you are willing to truly live a daily consecration of all that you are doing for Me only. Giving your will over to following My Will is a difficult sharing of control over your life. Another saintly characteristic is to have joy and full love of Me and others in your heart. A call to self-giving to help others without being asked is how saintly people live their lives. This is not an impossible feat, but with My grace you could live holier lives if you tried. That full commitment to love, know, and serve Me has been taught to you from your early years, and My call is always waiting for your answer. This is your goal, but even if you cannot be this saintly, striving for sainthood should still be your aspiration since this is the road to heaven. Struggling to not be controlled by earthly things and desires is a life long fight that will test you every day. Call on My help, the saints, and the angels, and we will come to you in your need."*

Later, at St. Theodore's Adoration I could see an orbiting satellite open up and it revealed a large laser gun for destroying other satellites. After it fired, it closed up to cover up what it was in space. Jesus said: *"My people, your countries rely heavily on transferring data, money, and voice communications by cell phone towers and satellites. If one country wanted to upset world trade and communications, they could*

*do so with a powerful satellite laser weapon which would have no ob-
structions in space to take out other important satellites. When solar
flares knocked out one satellite, there was great confusion in trying to
get a phone line through. Imagine what one laser could do to America
if it were aimed at all the specially orbited satellites right over your
country. These weapons have been in space many years, but they were
not meant to take down commercial satellites. This is just one more
way that America's economy is vulnerable in its dependency on communications."*

Wednesday, February 22, 2006: (Chair of St. Peter)

At St. Theodore's Adoration I could see a little wicker basket being carried by a young child. Jesus said: *"My people, I called the little children
to Me to make them an example of unfettered faith in love. They have*

*no fear because of
their age, and they
trust in their parents
to take care of them.
I want My people to
have the innocence
of a little child, and
to have faith in My
help as a child has
faith in their par-
ents. As you have
gone through life,
you have received
many gifts from Me
and I have protect-
ed you. My love
relationship with
everyone will never
change, and it is
you who diminish
in your love for Me.
My love for you is
constant, uncondi-
tional, and everlast-*

ing. Whether you are a serious sinner or nearly a saint, I will love you just the same, and wait for your repentance. Do not let worldly comforts and conveniences lead you away from Me. Loving and worshiping your Creator should be the greatest joy in life that you could share with Me. Come to Me with the faith of a child and you will be assured of a place in heaven."

Thursday, February 23, 2006:

At St. John the Evangelist after Communion I could see a large pool of water about waist high and people were drinking from it in joy. Jesus said: *"My people, this vision represents the people's thirst for My living water and not just earthly water that does not quench your thirst. Earthly water is a necessity to sustain the body, but you keep requiring to be filled again and often. My living water is My grace, peace, and rest which is a joy to quench your spiritual thirst for My Presence, and satisfy your stress with this life. Many people are restless in their spirit and they are not satisfied with the temporary comforts and pleasures of this life. Your soul is always seeking the peace of being with your Creator. Once you have a taste of My love, nothing else will satisfy you more. It is this spiritual peace with Me that you never want to leave. When your soul is purified from your sins in Confession, and when you receive Me in Holy Communion, this is the grace and peace of My living water. It is this spiritual peace that you should guard from all of the world's distractions. It is when you let the worldly things upset your peace that you become restless and agitated. It is only in love of Me and neighbor that you have peace, and not when you are angry and hostile toward others. Hate, anger, and revenge are the weapons of the evil one, and you cannot have peace with hate. So remove things in your life that cause you this stress, and only follow Me and things of love in your life. It is only when you keep your spiritual peace with Me that you can find this oasis of love in a world full of hate and violence. Come to Me always and I will satisfy you with My living water."*

Later, at the prayer group at Holy Name Adoration I could see a burning church building as someone had set it on fire on purpose. Jesus said: *"My people, recently you have seen ten or more churches destroyed by arson in the South. It has not been determined yet who is setting these fires. In Iraq the various religious factions have been destroying each other's mosques and holy sites. The evil one is behind racial and religious divisions, but it is unfortunate that houses of prayer are being destroyed. The hate in man is so great that he is defiling My houses. There is too much hate in the world and not enough love. You are to love everyone, even those who think different than you do."*

I could see some piles of wood and some organic wastes being used for alternate fuels. Jesus said: *"My people, you have seen how much America depends on foreign crude oil to run your cars and trucks with refined petroleum products. This high cost of oil and in politically difficult countries are the reasons for a good share of America's deficits between your imports over your exports. Even your president has been trying to push the development of alternate fuels. Developing noncarbon sources of fuel as wind, solar, hydrogen, and nuclear will take some time. Others are focused on ethanol from grain, but all of these fuels are a low percentage compared to oil products. This change from oil needs to be speeded up to improve your economy and your pollution."*

I could see a set of scales with various weights on either side. Jesus said: *"My people, many have taken various sides over your latest sale of some groups who want to control the operation of your Eastern ports. Some want more rigorous security checks over whoever runs these ports. Others are ashamed that foreigners are even allowed to control these port operations. Security in inspecting your cargo containers is very minimal and this lack of security is causing many investigations. Your country is having foreign investors spend your deficit dollars on your land, factories, and businesses. It is time to decide as a country how to balance your deficits, or foreigners will own more of your businesses than your own people, and you will be their servants."*

I could see some churches being renovated and old statues and decorations were being moved to the back of the church. Jesus said: *"My people, many renovations being made to My churches are being controlled by church leaders over objections of the parishioners. In some cases older churches need repair, but a majority are stripping My churches of many holy objects and are leaving plain walls and chairs instead of pews. I have warned My people to beware of this stripping of churches which is making way for New Age idols and statues. When you see such New Age teachings and idol worship enter a church, it is time to leave such churches for the coming underground church. In addition to burning churches, and fewer priests, you will have to endure this further divi-*

sion in My Church, but only for a short time before I will return and bring My victory over all evil."

I could see the inside of a building in the shape of a heart. Jesus said: *"My people, the violence of crime, wars, and abortions are all taking their toll on the fear and hopelessness that many people are enduring. It is hard to have loving communities when there is too much hate and little love in your people all over the world. Love starts with treating life as precious and avoiding all of this killing. You see a high divorce rate and living together outside of marriage as a sign of the immorality in all nations. If you cannot have peace and love in the family home, then how can you have love and peace in the world? Your wars are just a reflection of the divisions in the home boiling over into national relationships that are falling apart. Pray for peace first in your own homes, and for peace among all nations."*

I could see many disasters in earthquakes, mud slides, mine accidents, and roofs caving in. Jesus said: *"My people, you have seen a lot of deaths and injuries lately as people are being buried or trapped in various accidents and natural disasters. Several mining incidents have questioned safety conditions in the mines. Mud slides have questioned poor planning in removing trees or people living on flood plains. Some events can be prevented, but some are not planned. Pray for these affected families and help them with your donations if possible."*

I could see many hurricane devastated areas with little or no change because of contested insurance claims and government inactivity. Jesus said: *"My people, as reports are coming out of the failure of your levels of government to help the hurricane victims, various people are trying to shift the blame for not having a plan. Other victims are being forced out of their temporary shelters without any place to go. Your country can spend billions of dollars on wars and health problems, but it is hard to pay for these people in your own country who have lost everything. Again reach out to help them in donations and prayers."*

I could see some families having a hard time paying their bills with less paying jobs. Jesus said: *"My people, many of your good paying factory jobs and benefits are becoming a problem as jobs are shipped overseas or businesses are shutting down. It is not surprising to see your average wages decrease when your people need low paying service jobs to replace their factory jobs. Pray that your employers stop exporting your work just so the rich can gain more profits at the expense of your workers."*

Friday, February 24, 2006:

At St. John the Evangelist after Communion I could see some kind of device that was spinning out of control. Jesus said: *"My people, today's Gospel on marriage and divorce shows you how man's idea of divorce for convenience has not changed over the years. There is a pureness of love in a marriage as an institution and as a sacrament. I reminded My people then and now that I made you male and female to become one flesh as a life long commitment to each other. Many marry for physical love and when the attraction wanes, they want a different mate. You are more than the animals with reason and a soul, so every vocation, that you take on, should have more meaning than just a casual relationship. The home of a man and his wife is the proper environment of love for children to be brought up in. There are a lot of responsibilities in providing for a family, but you can call on My help for any financial or physical problems. There are many divorces in half of your marriages, but if you are united with Me in faith, you will have nothing to be concerned about. This self-giving love, that you are willing to share your life with someone, means that you will be tested by many temptations. It is a faith-filled person who perseveres in a marriage for the sake of the other spouse and the children. Children from divorced parents have to endure a stress-filled life, and they are the victims in divorce. Your society needs to treat life and marriage with sanctity in how precious they are. When people live in fornication without the blessing of marriage, they are not only sinning, but they lack the commitment both to Me and their mate. It is better to marry in the Church than to live a life of constant sin. Any other kind of marriage beside a man and a woman is a further abomination in My sight. I love everyone, but each of you decide your own way and one day you will have to make an accounting of your life at your judgment before Me. Unless you abide by My laws against adultery, fornication, and homosexual sins, you cannot enter the Kingdom of heaven. All sinners have to confess their sins and make a firm commitment to avoid this near occasion of sin. You can choose the road to heaven or the road to hell by your actions. Stay faithful to Me instead of satisfying your passions."*

Later, at St. Theodore's tabernacle I could see many faithful people walking to their refuges and at the same time I could see many black demons coming out of the ground to test the remaining souls. Jesus said: *"My people, a time of tribulation is coming when the Antichrist will declare himself, and evil people will take control of the world. This will be a time of trial when I have warned My faithful to call on Me, and your guardian angels will lead you to the nearest refuge. It will also be a time as in the vision when many demons will come out of the ground to harass those who are unprotected. You will need all of your blessed sacramentals and holy water to protect you from the evil ones. Trust in My help at that time to protect you just as I protected the Israelites from the Egyptian army. No matter how strong the evil ones will be, I will keep you safe from the taunts of the demons, and I will provide for your needs. Do not worry or have any fears of the evil ones because I will vanquish their power, and they will be chained in hell. I am always in control of things, and I am allowing this brief reign of the Antichrist to test your faith. You will be going through a living purgatory on earth, but your reward will be both in My Era of Peace and in heaven."*

Saturday, February 25, 2006:

At St. John the Evangelist after Communion I could see a scene of someone climbing up a mountain past some clouds to the top. Jesus said: *"My people, this vision of someone struggling up a mountain through the clouds to the top is like your struggle in life to come to heaven. Unless you can overcome your sins and seek My forgiveness, it is hard to advance on your path to heaven. Your desires for earthly things, that pass away, can hold you back in your climb for perfection. Even in today's Gospel I am asking you to have the faith of a little child to reach heaven. You are approaching the Lenten Season and this time of extra fasting and prayer should be an opportunity for you to gain extra graces by denying yourself of some earthly pleasures. By restricting the body, you can develop self-denial and come closer to Me doing good deeds and more Bible study. It is living what I teach you in the Scriptures that will be more important than memorizing chapter and verse. Reading My Gospels help keep your focus on climbing your own spiritual mountain to sainthood."*

Sunday, February 26, 2006:

At Holy Name after Communion I could see a pool of green water as it slowly darkened and faded away. Jesus said: *"My people, as you make your Lenten preparations, you are given your little mite boxes at church. Many people have plenty of money for their needs, but giving to charities on a regular basis is not every one's desire. During Lent you are encouraged to do more prayer and fasting, but also to think more of your almsgiving in helping people out of love and not just out of duty. All that you do during Lent should be done out of your own choosing to please Me and serve Me in helping others. Making a substantial gift to your favorite charity during the months of Lent could be one of your sacrifices instead of spending it on your own entertainment or more possessions that you do not need. If money is something that influences you too much, then letting go for a few donations could show your real sense of charity. The poor and hungry could use your help when you have more than enough surplus to share."*

Later, at St. Theodore's tabernacle I could see someone walking down the corridors of a hospital. Jesus said: *"My people, when you visit the sick, the elderly, or help someone, you are serving Me in them. For every good deed that you do for someone, you are storing up treasure in heaven for your judgment. The good that you do will balance off some of the punishment due for your sins. Take every opportunity to gain these graces when you can and you will not only be on a path to heaven, but even to a higher place in heaven. Many of the saints gave up all of their wealth and means for a living so they could live in full union with My Will in helping others. Trust in Me that I will always lead you to good things, while the evil one tempts you to waste your time on things that will not help your soul. The more you love people, the more willing you will be in helping them."*

Monday, February 27, 2006:

At St. John the Evangelist after Communion I could see a grain of wood going in one direction. Jesus said: *"My people, today's Gospel speaks of the problems in desiring money, but there are even deeper problems associated with pride, time and controlling your own will. Many people desire expensive possessions or the money that will buy them. Once these possessions are acquired, they soon grown old and obsolete and the need is now for something new. At times it is this desire for such temporary things that drives people's actions, even changing their priorities in life of loving Me and loving others. When you direct your life for your own selfish motives, then you are not choosing to follow My*

Will. You should not let any earthly desire control your life so much at the expense of forgetting about serving Me and Me in others. This vision of going against the grain means that you should not let your will cause so much disruption with others when you cannot have things go your own way. Pride can get in your way of loving Me and loving others. Your selfishness in sharing your time with others is similar to those who do not want to share their money with others. You must be generous with your time and money, as love should govern your actions more than your pride. Put your trust in Me and not in your money and possessions. Do not worry if you will have enough money for your needs because I will provide for your needs as I provide for the birds of the air."

Later, at St. Theodore's tabernacle I could see a dark, smooth sea and suddenly two good-sized waves came ashore one after the other and there was some severe water damage. Jesus said: *"My people, you have seen some substantial earthquakes in the last year, especially under water. These waves of water remind you of the damaging tsunami that killed several hundred thousand people. These waves are a sign that this could happen again and could even be triggered by your microwave devices. These waves travel hundreds of miles per hour and they strike very suddenly, even as you have seen damage from volcanoes and mud slides. Many preparations and warning systems have been put in place to warn you of an impending tsunami, but you will need to get to high ground quickly. Pray that any more of these natural disasters will not be so deadly or damaging as your Hurricane Katrina."*

Tuesday, February 28, 2006:

At Holy Name after Communion I could see a daylight scene and then a dark night scene. Jesus said: *"My people, today's Gospel speaks about those who follow Me may have to suffer persecution. There is also consolation for those who are downtrodden by others that the first will be last and the last will be first. In today's society there is no justice because those with money control the judges and sway the juries. Even in your country if you speak out against war, abortions, or homosexuality, you will suffer persecution and even lose your jobs. Powerful interests by lobbyists and the one world people are behind how your government is run and how they dictate to the people. But it is your courts that are using liberal judges to strike down your laws ban-*

ning abortions and pornography. Many of your courts are legislating immorality against the will of the people. It is for these condemning rulings that your country has suffered natural disasters and you will continue to suffer until you are brought to your knees. You will not see justice until I return and cast all of these evil doers into hell, but My faithful will see My new heavens and new earth in My Era of Peace. Do not worry about the dark days of this tribulation, but look forward to My victory when My faithful will be vindicated."

Later, at St. Theodore's Adoration I could see a small model of a beautiful church and then I saw a small doll house with some small pieces of furniture of a child's toys. Jesus said: *"My people, your old churches are a lot more pleasing to Me than your new and remodeled churches that appear to have no life. In older days the parishioners actually helped to build their local churches and the people were strong in their faith because of their love of the Sacred. Today, you are concerned in getting awards for your builder than having a strong belief in your faith. The more simple your faith as a little child, the more powerful your faith will be. Many changes in destroying My altars have the people protesting these structures, and this has brought division in My Church. I call My people not to give up their faith over these changes, but realize that it is another sign of My coming Remnant Church where eventually you will have to flee to My refuges. Once you are there, you will be protected from all harm and I will feed you My holy Bread until I return."*

March 1, 2006: (Ash Wednesday)

At Holy Name after Communion I could see Jesus kneeling and praying in the desert as He prepared for His public ministry. Jesus said: *"My people, this first day of Lent is focused on the saying of the priest:* 'Remember thou are dust, and unto dust thou shalt return.' *This expression of ashes is to humble everyone to the fact that I created you from the elements of the earth, and when you die, your body will return to dust and ashes. Lent is a special time of the year to put the spiritual life of your soul in proper perspective to where you will go after your death. While you are here in this life on earth, you should be preparing your soul for heaven before you die. The idea of a forty day period of prayer and fasting comes from My preparation for My public ministry after I was baptized by St. John the Baptist. During the year there are many distractions that can lead you astray from your strong fervor of loving*

Me and your neighbor as yourself. By an extra focus on fasting between meals, doing some penances of giving up something you like, and an increase in your prayers as the daily Liturgy of the Hours, you can help purify your life of earthly desires. Many times your craving for things in addictions, or other habits that consume your time, draw you away from Me. Just as I fasted and prayed in the desert, it was a time to resist Satan's temptations of eating bread, throwing Myself over a cliff, and bowing down to him in worship. In all of these temptations I quoted Scripture to him in answer to his taunts. You are going to be tested also by Satan's temptations every day of your life. So take advantage of this Lenten Season to build up your resistance to his temptations."

Later, at St. Theodore's Adoration I could see an antenna and there was a light pulsating and emanating periodically from the antenna. Jesus said: *"My people, this pulsing beacon of light represents microwave signals being sent over an area in the sky. In combination with the materials placed in the sky by chem trails, these microwave pulses could trigger epidemic diseases in given areas. The evil ones are causing fear with threats of epidemics. Even worse, they are instigating these viruses and diseases on purpose to lower the population, and give cause for declaring emergencies and martial law. The evil ones will use any tactics to take away your freedoms and give the evil people control over everyone. As the evil ones begin to take over, My angels will lead you to My refuges where you will be healed of all diseases by drinking the spring water at the refuges and looking on My luminous cross over each refuge. Trust in My protection and My healing and the evil ones will not be able to harm you or find you."*

Thursday, March 2, 2006:

At St. John the Evangelist after Communion I could see some singers in the foreground and many people in a stadium behind them. Jesus said: *"My people, in the first reading about Moses (Deut. 30: 17-19) he is giving the Israelites his parting blessing as they are about to enter the Promised Land from their forty years in the desert. His address on choosing life is a good lesson for every nation, especially America.* 'If, however, you turn away your hearts and will not listen (to God), but are led astray and adore and serve other gods, I tell you now that you will certainly perish. I have set before you life and death, the blessing and the curse. Choose life, then, that you and your descendants may live, by loving the Lord, your God, heeding His voice, and holding fast to Him.' *Right now you are serving the gods of money, possessions, lust, and war. The morals of following My laws have been replaced by your greed for money and pleasures. The moral decay in your society can be seen in your movies, your actions, and your laws. Because you have chosen this path of sin instead of following My laws, you must accept the consequences that are leading to your destruction as a nation. There are evil rich people who are controlling your government and your money that are leading you to bankruptcy both physically and morally. This is their plan for takeover, but your people are so steeped in their sins and pleasures, they do not see the coming loss of your freedoms. All of the natural disasters and your deficits will bring your people to their knees unless your people repent of their sins and worship your Creator instead of created things."*

Later, at the prayer group at Holy Name Adoration I could see some gambling wheels at a casino in the South. Jesus said: *"My people, New Orleans has only a quarter of its original population after the hurricanes. Yet they are still celebrating a sinful carnival atmosphere along with the new gambling casinos. The people here were brought to their knees, and they still have not linked this destruction with their sinful lifestyles. Where sin abounds flagrantly, you can expect My wrath to fall on those unrepentant sinners. Pray for the citizens of these destroyed cities that they repent and call on My help to recover."*

I could see someone driving that was getting upset with slow and aggressive drivers. Jesus said: *"My people, this Lent is a time to try and improve your lives even in the little things as driving your car. It is easy to get upset over slow drivers, or those that are distracted by cell phones. The real challenge is to keep your peace and do not let the little things get you angry and disturbed. If you are tempted to overreact to such things as driving problems, then say some prayers at that time to calm your emotions. Carry this same thought into every situation that could disturb your peace."*

I could see a lot of debris at the side of the road. Jesus said: *"My people, when you make up your mind to clean out your garage or basement, you make the extra effort to get rid of those things that are no longer needed. Your souls need to be cleansed of your sins more than just cleaning out some trash. If you have been sinning for a long time without Confession, it is difficult to see how badly you need repentance and My forgiveness. You need to recognize that all of you are sinners and are in need of frequent Confession. Make an effort especially during Lent to get to Confession at least once a month, even if you have not committed any serious sin. Pray for all souls to repent and return to My forgiving heart of love. You need to have pure souls to get into heaven, so take the condition of your soul seriously and keep it ready and pure for the day that I will call you home."*

I could see a shark with sharp teeth searching the waters. Jesus said: *"My people, you are aware of the dangers of a shark when you are in the water because you can see their fins. Many do not always see the danger of the evil ones in their temptations to serious sin. Because the devil is crafty and deceiving, you need to be on your guard against sin at all times. This is why daily prayer and frequent reception of the sacraments are a great help to keep you strong against temptations. Look at the lives of the saints and seek to imitate them in their holiness. Do not have fear of the evil ones because when you have Me for you, who could be against you?"*

I could see someone store some money in the bank and some other valuables in a safe deposit box. Jesus said: *"My people, you are very careful to guard your valuables and have all manners of security devices in your homes and cars. Why do you take such care of your earthly things, but you care little to store up heavenly treasures of your prayers and good deeds? I have told you many times that where your treasure lies, is also where your heart lies. You cannot love both Me and money at the same time. Put your trust in Me and worship Me instead of your money."*

I could see some prison bars at the gates of a prison. Jesus said: *"My people, when you commit a crime of theft or shoot someone, you expect the police to bring you to justice and finally to prison. This is a consequence of your sinful actions against society. When you commit sins against My Commandments, you also must expect that you will have to make reparation for your sins. When you are in serious sin, you may not see the bars of a prison, but the bonds of your sins can keep you from coming to your spiritual potential. You always can do more in your life to improve your holiness, but you must have the faith and determination to move forward in a better life. I love you always, even in your sinful actions. Make an extra effort in this Lent to loosen the bonds of your earthly desires that hold you as a prisoner."*

I could see a raging fire along some prairie land. Jesus said: *"My people, America continues to be tested by 100 mph winds, fires, and snow storms. Many of these events are signs for those with eyes to see that you are getting closer to the end times. Your ongoing wars and insurrection are taking lives all over the world, even as different religious views have brought some divisions. Love should be uppermost in your mind and it is better to strive to build up society as peace makers than to let hate and war destroy any peace present. Work and pray to stop your wars where greed and pride will gain you nothing."*

Friday, March 3, 2006:

At St. John the Evangelist after Communion I could see a strong pillar holding up a part of a house. Jesus said: *"My people, many of you are strong in your faith, but even more around you are lukewarm, or not even religious at all. My faithful remnant are the pillars of My Church and you need to give good example to your family members and those around you. If you are to be models for others to follow, you need to stay strong in your faith by renewing yourself with the discipline of your Lenten devotions. By extra prayer and fasting, you can nourish and build up your faith so you will be strong against temptations to sin. You all are subject to temptations every day, so everyone needs a time of Lent as a retreat from your worldly cares and distractions. Take this time to grow in your faith instead of accepting the status quo. Unless you keep gaining in your perfection, it will require more purgatory to cleanse your earthly desires."*

Later, at St. Theodore's tabernacle I could see an assembly line where they make cars. Jesus said: *"My people, many of your factories are having a difficult time in matching quality and price for your durable goods as cars and other high value products. The lost market share is bringing many of your companies close to bankruptcy with many layoffs as well. It is hard to blame your consumers for wanting to buy better quality and cheaper products. You are turning into sellers instead of makers, and your manufacturing jobs are declining steadily. If your government does not limit these imports and the balance of trade deficits, you will be exporting your money and the ownership of all of your businesses. This is another area where the overhead of all of your taxes, benefits, and labor costs are pricing you out of your global marketplace. Pray to Me for helping you in your jobs and keeping your employment to feed your families. Your morals also need to improve as well as your coming to Me for repentance of your sins."*

Saturday, March 4. 2006:

At St. John the Evangelist after Communion I could see a picture in a frame and the glass was broken. Jesus said: *"My people, I want to call your attention to the fact that all of you are sinners with faults, and you all need to come to Me in repentance of your sins. Do not be dismayed at your weaknesses, but be thankful that you have a Savior who loves you and wants you to reach out for My help to be holy. Do not criticize people for their faults because everyone is in various stages of progress in their faith and learning experience. By being loving and willing to assist people, you will keep the peace instead of making them resentful of your criticism. At the same time you must be loving when people criticize you and not be prideful in getting angry at someone's remarks. Even when people are slow or forgetful, resist showing up other's faults just because you are faster or have a better memory. Many arguments start with unnecessary criticism, and both parties need to be more understanding of each other's faults. When you think to criticize someone, remind yourself how others see your faults and are offended also. Think love in your actions and comments, and you will spread My loving peace instead of being a bad example to others. If you truly love Me and your neighbor, you will think twice the next time you are quick to judge someone."*

Later, at St. Theodore's tabernacle I could see a large drainage ditch being built and there was a large hole into a septic sewer that was in the middle of the ditch. Jesus said: *"My people, this problem of handling flash flooding from heavy downpours also threatens to carry untreated sewer water into your rivers and lakes. The bad quality of the water in New Orleans caused burns and rashes for those who walked in it. These large rainfalls from violent storms are going to be more frequent. In California unusual rains are causing further mud slides. Your storms are partly increasing in violence and rainfall because of the higher temperatures in the Gulf of Mexico and the oceans. Your country is going to have to make plans to deal with more disasters like Hurricane Katrina. Living near these Southern states is going to be more of a liability than vacation sites. America is suffering in more ways from your natural disasters in part due to your immoral behavior and your lack of repentance for your sins."*

Sunday, March 5, 2006:

At Holy Name after Communion I could see someone kneeling in prayer in a dim lit church. Jesus said: *"My people, your deacon today touched on all the Lenten devotions that the people need to be doing to be holier people and take advantage of this Lenten opportunity of grace. Some may want to attend some daily Masses as an extra penance. Daily prayer is a good way to stay in close communication and express your love for Me more than once a week. Stations of the Cross help you to understand My suffering for each of you and they prepare you for Holy Week. Fasting from food between meals and having a modest seafood dinner on Fridays helps you to train your body to fight the devil's temptations. The most important Lenten suggestion is to confess your sins at least once a month, even throughout the year. You all are sinners and in need of My forgiveness. In Confession I cleanse your sins and fill your soul with grace. When healed of serious sin, you are made alive and your spiritual life is renewed in your love relationship with Me. I mentioned almsgiving in previous messages, but it is also a way to be humble in healing your pride and any love of money by sharing with your favorite charities. All of these devotions have one goal of strengthening your soul and faith on your path to heaven."*

Monday, March 6, 2006:

At St. John the Evangelist after Communion I could see a canyon and people holding shields for protection. Jesus said: *"My people, this vision of people carrying shields is all about the battles against evil that you must bear every day. There are three sources of evil in your life. You are tempted by your peers to follow the crowd, even if it involves sinful behavior, or you may risk social rejection. You are tempted by the devil just as I was tempted in the desert. The devil is very cunning and deceptive in his temptations and distractions from things that are holy. You also are tempted by your own will in your earthly desires, and sometimes even addictions or habitual sins. Knowing and understanding your sources of sin can prepare you for these attacks so you are not found unaware. In all of these temptations pray for My help and do not give in to these sins which you rationalize as unimportant. Every time that you sin, you are offending Me, and you need to come to Me in Confession for forgiveness and seek My mercy. I will always forgive you, cleanse your sins, and fill your soul with My grace. By having strong faith and a strong prayer life, you will have a spiritual shield of protection from all of the evil that you will face each day."*

Later, at St. Theodore's tabernacle I could see a lot of people in a van traveling on the road. Jesus said: *"My people, many times people travel on vacation during the summer time. This vacation trip has taken on a different purpose as if you are practicing for the days when you will have to leave for My refuges in the rural areas. Once you leave the cities and suburbs, it quickly changes to thinly populated areas. The more you can do a little camping and practice using your backpack materials, you can get a preview of what it would be like at a refuge. Do not worry about your needs because I will provide for you and your protection. My angels will keep you from being seen and My luminous cross over the refuges will heal all of your diseases and infirmities. So the next time that you take a vacation in the car, think of how prepared you are to leave for My refuges, because that time will be coming sooner than you think."*

Tuesday, March 7, 2006:

At Holy Name after Communion I could see a globe of the earth as people were praying their prayers. Jesus said: *"My people, I taught My apostles the Our Father as a way to pray to God. Prayer is an important part of your spiritual life, and in reverence you should pray slowly and think of what you are saying. There are various reasons for prayer. You pray to give Me Adoration and it is your way of saying how much you love Me. You pray over things and people to bless them. At meals you pray that you are thankful for your food, and that it may be safe to eat. You pray over people to call on My healing and sometimes to release them from demons. You pray many times prayers of petition or intercession for saving souls from going to hell, souls in purgatory, peace in the world, and a stoppage of all the killing going on all over the world. You pray to thank Me for all of your blessings of things and graces of faith, as well as for all the people that I place in your life. The ultimate prayer of Thanksgiving is the prayer of the Mass and My gift of Myself to you in Holy Communion. You also pray to Me in asking forgiveness of your sins, and you are willing to make reparation for your sins by your prayers, as in your penance after Confession. In all of these ways you are humbling yourself before Me as you are reaching out to enrich your love relationship with Me. Every prayer is heard and I will answer whatever is best for your soul or others in My time."*

Later, at St. Theodore's Adoration I could see Jesus suffering on the cross for me and my sins. Jesus said: *"My people, there are times in your life when old habits or addictions can control your life in either repetitive sin or things that waste your time. As soon as you allow one little opening, as a drunk takes one drink, you can open the floodgates to the things that can control you. When your desire for these earthly cares so consumes you, it is hard to break the chain of this desire. It is sometimes better if you refuse to be enticed the first time and remove any occasions that would lead you to sin or a return to a bad habit. You*

are not alone in this battle of control over your life. When you come to Me in prayer, I am at your side to help you break the bonds of any control that addictions or bad habits have over you. You need to let this desire go in order to be free of its control over you. Take up reading some good spiritual books and this could take your mind off of your desires. Only by freeing yourself of these earthly desires can you begin to grow in your perfection that you are seeking to enter heaven. Give your life over to what I want you to do, and

your spiritual peace will return to you free of the controls of the world's money, possessions, and fame. Search harder for your freedom and peace with Me, and your soul will be satisfied in getting close to your Lord. I conquered all sin and all things are possible with Me. You must make that forward motion to love Me and put My plan for you as your top priority. Love Me and your neighbor as yourself, and love will overcome all of your earthly faults."

Wednesday, March 8, 2006:

At Holy Name after Communion I could see a winding sidewalk path through a public set of buildings. Jesus said: *"My people, today's Gospel and the Reading talk about Jonah in Nineveh, and I tell My people of that time that I am greater than Jonah and Solomon. (Luke 11:29-32) When Jonah was called to send a message of repentance to Nineveh, he was reluctant at first. His message was actually taken up seriously as the people repented of their sins and their city was spared destruction. In most other accounts the people refused My call to repentance and in the flood with Noah and the fire against Sodom and Gomorrah, My judgment fell against these people. I give the people of every generation fair warning of their sinful lives, and if they refuse to follow My ways, as the Israelites, their towns will be destroyed and they will fall into captivity. As with Me and most of the prophets, the people do not want to be reprimanded to repent and change their lives of earthly comforts and pleasures. So I tell all of My prophets to not be disappointed if people refuse to listen to your words. But remember that if you have been given a mission, it is still your responsibility to speak out to save souls by asking them to repent and change their lives. If My messengers follow My call, then they will save their souls and those who listen. Those, who refuse to follow My Commandments and do not accept Me into their lives, are calling this condemnation of the people of Nineveh upon themselves. As this evil age grows worse, My faithful remnant will be few in number who are proclaiming their love for Me. You see the immorality all around you and many are no longer praying or attending Mass. Do not be discouraged about the few in number of My true believers, but be faithful to your own faith, and reach out to save as many souls as possible."*

Later, at St. Theodore's Adoration I could see a crossroads of three main roads. Jesus said: *"My people, this picture of some crossroads signifies that America is at a crossroads in making any more decisions for making war with Iran. The secret deal to sell the operations of your ports to the Arabs was a payoff for using their airport for future military uses. Now your Vice President and Secretary of State are laying down the rhetoric for a war with Iran if they do not stop their intent on making nuclear weapons. The American people want out of your war in Iraq, and surely do not want another war with Iran. Your Congress needs to assert its authority over who declares war, and who can sell the operations of your ports, or your country will be openly controlled by the one world people. You already have seen what a disaster attacking Iraq has brought America, so why should you continue this madness by starting another war in Iran? Pray for a stoppage of your wars now that could possibly lead to a world war if Russia and China defend Iran."*

Thursday, March 9, 2006:

At St. John the Evangelist after Communion I could see some lips talking in secret, but I could not see the faces. Jesus said: *"My people, the one world people are behind the scenes preparing for another war in Iran. The oil stakes are too high for them in the Middle East to allow politics to get in their way. These are the central bankers and the rich controlling all of your governments to follow their directions. I have told you before that the bankers make money on the interest of your war debts that are now eight trillion dollars, and they profit from selling arms to both sides. War is big business and a money maker for them, and that is why they are encouraging this war with Iran. The unexpected consequences of such a war could be worse than the debacle in Iraq, if more countries are involved. Such a war would send oil prices higher and cause a world wide problem with oil supplies. Pray much that such a war does not take place, or many lives could be lost. If this war occurs, you will have proof of who is running your governments."*

Later, at the prayer group at Holy Name Adoration I could see Jesus traveling with His cross on His way to Calvary. Jesus said: *"My people, you are seeing before you some Lenten symbols in some new Stations of the Cross and a picture of how I suffered with My crown of thorns. These traditional symbols help to add some reality to how I suffered for each one of you. When you walk My Stations of the Cross, it is how you can share your suffering with My own suffering. I am still suffering on the cross for your current sins that are continuing. Give praise and glory to Me for giving My life so that you could live a free spiritual life today. During Lent you could read the Stations of the Cross as one of your devotions to Me."*

I could see some muddy water on one of the docks of your ports. Jesus said: *"My people, your president was shocked by the reaction of your Congress to putting down his selling of the port operations to an Arab shipping concern. The real security risk was voiced by your people, and the future elections*

pushed your Congressmen and women to act to protect their jobs. Your Congress has opened up a whole new look at how little these containers are inspected for nuclear or other dangerous materials. It is one of the first times that Congress has asserted itself against foreign big business."

I could see some empty seats at the top of your government. Jesus said: *"My people, this rejection of the Arabs to run your ports is just the beginning of a challenge to your president on many issues that his own party is distancing from him. The war in Iraq which has cost hundreds of billions of dollars has grown colder in its support. A possible new war in Iran could be another area of disagreement. The one world people are finally meeting some resistance to having things their own way. Keep praying for peace and that nuclear arms are not used."*

I could see some of the simple dwellings of the people in the Middle East. Jesus said: *"My people, this area where I lived has a real contrast in the old city of Jerusalem vs. the newer city. There are still many sacred traditions carried on by the Jews, the Palestinians, and the Christians. These peoples have tried to live together, but there are still clashes over the ownership of the land. There will never be total peace, but some of the recent changes are helping the peace."*

I could see some open windows along an enclosed stairway. Jesus said: *"My people, as your time moves on, there are more people wanting peaceful diplomatic solutions instead of more wars. There are different opinions, but preventing war is easier to strive for than all of the destruction and killing in a war. It is greed for land, oil, and control that has driven some countries to even think that they could win and profit from war. With nuclear weapons in so many hands, war on that scale does not seem worth it. Pray that proper thinking will prevail with no war."*

I could see some people praying and going to Confession. Jesus said: *"My people, you have just completed your first week of Lent and it would be good to look at how your initial intentions are working out. Some have adopted some fasting and extra prayers, but are you being successful in your plans? If you have yet to start a Lenten regimen, now would be a good time to implement some things that would improve your spiritual life. If you already are falling away from your original intentions, it is not too late to get back to your Lenten devotions. Think of how much that I suffered for you, and you could think of sharing some penances for Me."*

I could see some people putting some money in their mite boxes. Jesus said: *"My people, I mentioned how almsgiving should be a more important part of your Lenten sacrifices. If your means permit, it would be a good exercise to make a good donation to your favorite charity during each month of Lent which is only two months. You are working to improve your spiritual life, so helping others would be an appropriate Lenten suffering. When you help others, you are helping Me."*

Friday, March 10, 2006:

At St. John the Evangelist after Communion I could see a safety net as for performers in high flying acrobats. Jesus said: *"My people, this vision of a safety net for acrobats is how you should see Me in your life. Many people are very apprehensive to take risks in life out of fear of losing their jobs, or not being able to provide for their living needs. You have read in the Scriptures* (Matt. 6:26-29) *many times about having trust in Me because I feed the birds of the air and dress the lilies of the field. If I can take care of these things of nature, how much more value are you in My eyes that I will provide for your needs. Man is always worried if he cannot see an immediate solution for his survival. I am that safety net behind you. You need to trust in My help for your jobs and the food and clothing that you need. In addition to helping you with your physical needs, I am also a safety net for your spiritual needs as well. At times you fall into sin, but I am there to lift you up in Confession. It is you who must recognize your faults and seek My forgiveness. With sorrow and reparation for your sins, then I can replenish your soul with grace and cleanse your sins from your souls. I am always here to forgive you, if you would just see your need for My grace. With this faith and trust in Me for both your physical and spiritual needs, then you can be at peace that your Lord is watching over you in every little thing of your life."*

Later, at St. Theodore's tabernacle I could see an octagonal shaped chapel and there was a scene of a large giant as in David and Goliath. Jesus said: *"My people, at times you face almost impossible tasks as when David faced Goliath in combat. But David had faith in God and he trusted Him to help fight his battle. When David fell the giant with his sling shot and stone, David was not surprised at his victory, but he was confident in his Lord's help. This deep trust in God is how all of My faithful should also be confident in My help in all of your trials. Do not be surprised at your success, but give Me praise and glory for answering your prayers. Sometimes you let your fears stifle you from accomplishing My mission for your life. I have empowered you with the power of the Holy Spirit to do great feats to prove to you about the power of the Holy Spirit. The more you see My power manifested, it should embolden you to evangelize souls for My sake. Remember to trust in Me, and I will accomplish great things through you, just as I enabled David to conquer Goliath."*

Saturday, March 11, 2006:

At St. John the Evangelist after Communion I could see the United

States from up high and a dark shadow of evil came over the country starting from the East. Jesus said: *"My people, this dark shadow of evil, that will come over your country, is coming from the Antichrist who will live in Europe as he takes over the European Union. The central bankers will sponsor the Antichrist as he will promise them power. Once in power the Antichrist will do away with all of his sponsors and leaders, and replace them with demon-inspired people as himself. The father of lies will entice people to work for him and then he will force them to worship him and accept his mark of the beast. He will do away with the United States on his way to world domination. Pray for My help during this evil reign, and I will protect My faithful remnant at My refuges."*

Sunday, March 12, 2006:

At Holy Name after Communion I could see Jesus walking slowly with a young child for several minutes as a movie. Jesus said: *"My people, you have heard Me talk about those who harm or give bad example to My little ones and how they need to be punished severely. I will forgive those who repent, but there is still more reparation for these sins because they can mislead an innocent soul. Those, who beat children or even kill them as in abortion, will have even more to answer for. Parents and grandparents need to protect their children from bad influences from bad movies, bad TV programs, internet searching in bad subjects, and even bad influences from their friends. It is not easy to be watching over them every moment, but the parents need to know what they are watching and doing in these areas. There are many worldly bad influences that can corrupt the minds of your children. You cannot depend on your society to protect your little ones, but you must be pro-active on your part and looking out for your children's interests. This is a physical and spiritual protection that you need to put around your little ones. Remember on your day of judgment that you will have to answer to Me on how you worked to save the souls of your children."*

Later, at St. Cecilia's tabernacle I could see several people riding bicycles when there was not much fuel. Jesus said: *"My people, I have warned you about preparing to go to refuges for protection and for food, water, and healing. In addition to the things for your backpacks, I also have asked you to have some good running bikes handy in case you are having a fuel shortage. As the chips will be used for buying and selling, you will not want to use chips to buy gas. Many wars are occurring where the oil is pumped, and there are many terrorists trying to sabotage oil lines. Now even Iran is threatening an oil shortage if sanctions are placed on them for working on nuclear bombs. You may also have to buy some helmets to be legal on the road. With some crude transportation, My angels can lead you to safety at My refuges."*

Monday, March 13, 2006:

At Holy Name after Communion I could see someone in the process of dying and it was difficult for the family. Jesus said: *"My people, when people die from cancer or strokes, it can be a trying time for care givers and the family. Some prefer to be at home, hospices, or special places at hospitals. This kind of death is a slow process, but it may give the dying person a chance to receive Confession and the Anointing of the Sick before they pass. Remember also to be praying for these souls because the devil tempts you to reject Me, even until you die. Having the sacraments before you die is always reassuring to the family that you had a chance to make your peace with Me before your judgment. It is also comforting to the family for friends and relatives to visit the dying person before the end, as well as at the funeral. Your life is valuable and paying your respects before death is just as important as after death. Friends should be willing to offer their services in helping the care givers when possible. Prayers and good deeds are appreciated greatly by the family, and they store up treasures in heaven for your love and concern."*

Later, at Our Lady of Lourdes after Communion I could see a door open and Jesus came in. Jesus said: *"My people, when you come to Me in prayer, you must concentrate on opening your heart to Me. You have pride of all kinds holding you back from fully letting go of earthly confidence and desires. If you are the least little embarrassed, you are defensive with explanations. You must admit to yourself that you all have faults and just let your pride pass. You may even have spiritual pride as the Pharisees who thought they had all of the answers about God. You need to be open to want to learn more about Me, even if it comes from someone else. Once you can give your will over to following My Will, you can remove this spiritual pride that can keep the door closed to your heart. When you can accept yourself as nothing in My Presence, then My love can reach deeper into your heart and soul.*

When you can let go of your pride, you will be able to embrace My love and My peace. You are the only one who can open the door to My love, so reach out for My helping hand so I can lead you to heaven."

Tuesday, March 14, 2006:

At Holy Name after Communion I could see a lot of wind and objects were flying all around me. Jesus said: *"My people, during the change of seasons from winter to spring, you usually see more violent wind damage as with tornadoes. Each storm system at this time of year brings dramatic temperature changes which generate large pressure changes. Tornadoes and fires have been ravaging your middle of the country with lost lives and great damage. Many of these disasters are a wake-up call to how vulnerable you are to these storms. This world is passing away and you should not get too comfortable with all of your earthly possessions because they can be taken away with one storm. Rather focus and trust in Me because I am never changing, and your eternal destination is more important than any of your earthly concerns. Be willing to accept losses in your possessions as they are only temporary. Even the lives around you are being taken home as well, so you have had to suffer the loss of loved ones who are Mine also. Accept whatever comes into your life, and be thankful for all that you have and the gift of lives that are with you just for a time and are taken. This life is short and you need to live it in love while you are still here."*

Later, at St. Theodore's Adoration I could see an old wooden house in a Western town with a wooden sidewalk. Jesus said: *"My people, some people are fortunate to have a modest dwelling for a home. During your life you pay a mortgage, taxes, and utilities just to have a roof over your head. Remember in My public life that I stayed as a guest with people and I did not have a house of My own. Some priests and nuns take a vow of poverty to live simply in convents or rectories. Many saints did not have a house of their own either. The more you own, the harder it will be to give up these things before you die. All of your possessions are only temporary and you are like a steward, but not the owner. It is the same even with your life and soul. You are a part of My creation and when you die, I am taking My creation back home to Me for judgment. You can reject Me by your free will choice, but your soul is drawn to My love in being your Creator. Trust in Me with all that you have been given, and be willing to consecrate everything of things and loved ones over to Me. Then you will be in the right disposition to come to heaven by emptying yourself of all of your earthly desires."*

Wednesday, March 15, 2006:

At Holy Name after Communion I could see a very large church with a huge dome and a high ceiling. Jesus said: *"My people, in the Gospel I talked about the Pharisees and the leaders of the Church who loved places of honor. Even today your people strive for places of fame and distinction at places of dinners and banquets. Many of your politicians and Hollywood stars are looking to get elected or receive distinguished awards. When two of My apostles sought heavenly distinction, I told them that it was not Mine to give, but they needed to be the servants of everyone. Do not be driven by pride for man's awards and honors, for I see in secret all that you are doing, and you would rather be rewarded in heaven for your deeds than here on earth. In another parable about places at a wedding table I told the people that it is better to take a lower place and be raised up higher, than to take an honored place and later have to go to the back. Those, who exalt themselves, will be humbled, but those, who humble themselves, will be exalted."*

Later, at St. Theodore's Adoration I could look out at a farm field full of crops. Jesus said: *"My people, the small farmers in your country are slowly disappearing because they cannot compete against the larger farms, and they are more vulnerable to bad crop seasons, or low prices for their crops. Think of the expenses of barns, tractors, feed, seed, and fertilizer, and it is difficult to manage these costs and make a living for the family. There are various subsidies, but even these aids are slowly disappearing and are causing farmers bankruptcy, or a selling off of their lands. The more small farmers are retiring, the more big farms will control your prices in the hands of a few. You need to pray for these small farmers because together they produce a good share of the food that you eat."*

I could see a picture of our back yard where the tomatoes and raspberries were grown. Jesus said: *"My people, this deceased neighbor of yours, Cecilia, had a deep love for gardening and living things and animals. She was very sensitive to Jocelyn and your family as neighbors. She had some difficulties in her last days, but she was a very good woman and neighbor. She wishes to thank her daughter and all of her care givers for helping her in her last days. She received a blessing from*

Father Ted and she was thankful for the sacraments that she received, as well as the Holy Communions from your wife. She is resting in a better place and she wants to tell her family not to worry about her. She loves all of you and she will be praying for you. She also prays that her family will work out their affairs in love and according to her wishes."

Thursday, March 16, 2006:

At St. John the Evangelist after Communion I could see an opening into reality that showed how people were suffering and it went beneath outward appearances. Jesus said: *"My people, today's Gospel about Divies, the rich man, and Lazarus, the beggar, is a lesson in the sin of omission. At times you are rushing through life a little too fast to stop and notice how those people around you are hurting. It is true that most people do not have the finances to help all of those that you meet and are in need. But most people can afford some kind of donation of time and money to help the poor, or one of your relatives that are in need. It is hard and even callous to ignore the poor and needy around you, even if you can only donate groceries for your local food shelf for the poor. Some even donate their time in feeding soup to the homeless. Remember at the judgment I will ask you if you helped Me in the hungry, the thirsty, the sick, or the dying. For those, who cared for Me in the poor and the needy, I will welcome you into My heavenly banquet. For those, who did not care for Me in these poor of the world, you could be led to the same place of torment as this rich man. For all of you have been gifted with My Word and the prophets, and if you refused to listen to Me and them, then you have chosen your possible fate in hell as well as this rich man."*

Later, at the prayer group at Holy Name Adoration I could see a crucifix with little steps going down both sides of a hill. Jesus said: *"My people, this picture of a crucifix at the top of a hill is a reminder to all of My people how during Lent you are all walking in My footsteps to your own Calvary. It is not easy to bear suffering in this life, but each person is asked to pick up your daily cross and follow Me. Some are better able to carry their cross, while others need to call more on My help as Simon helped carry My cross. You will never be tested beyond what you are capable of suffering. Join all of your troubles and suffering with My suffering on the cross. The hope that keeps My followers going is that one day you could be with Me in heaven and even in your resurrected body."*

I could see the Light of Jesus radiate out from the tomb and these light rays burned an image of Jesus onto the Shroud of Turin. Jesus said: *"My people, this image of Light, that radiated out from My tomb, is how I was physically resurrected in the body as a glorious beautiful body, as I showed My three disciples in My Transfiguration. I told My apostles that I would rise from the dead after three days in the tomb. This was a hard saying since no one has ever resurrected from the dead before. In today's Gospel the rich man said: 'What if someone would come from the dead? Then they would believe.' I rose from the dead and still there are unbelievers. Believe that I truly resurrected, just as all souls, who believe, will also be resurrected."*

I could again see people carrying their crosses. Jesus said: *"My people, many people want to go directly to the Resurrection, but you first must suffer your own Good Friday. This life is difficult to endure and at times some are wondering how long will it take for Jesus to return and defeat the evil ones. Some are even getting impatient with Me and think My coming is a long way off. Let Me assure you that it will happen in your lifetime. Each day during Lent offer up all of your prayers and fasting to help save your soul and the souls of those that you are praying for."*

I could see someone kneeling in prayer before a picture of (Jesus). Jesus said: *"My people, Lent is a time for conversions and retreats as you are sorrowing for having offended Me with your sins. It is a time of repentance and a time of retrospection on how you can improve your spiritual life. If you do not come out of Lent spiritually refreshed, then you have not worked hard to purge your bad habits out of your life. Learn from your Lenten experience and see how you can apply your learning to live better and holier lives."*

I could see some people visiting a monastery to learn more about living a simpler life. Jesus said: *"My people, some have gone to monasteries to view the quiet and rigors of living a monastic life of rededicating their lives to Me. When you fast, pray, and live life in a simple cell, it is a way of coming closer to Me without the distractions of the world pulling you down. The worldly life puts many demands on your time and at times you need to ask yourself if you are really fulfilling the mission that I have given you. Prayer is a powerful weapon in your fight against the temptations of the devil. See the need for frequent Confession to keep you humble, and keep your focus on Me as you walk on your way to your Calvary."*

I could see someone praying in their prayer room. Jesus said: *"My people, even though it is good to go to a retreat at a monastery for a weekend, you still are living in the world, but you do not have to be of the world. You can have a mini-retreat every day that you take a little time to pray in your prayer room or at church before My Blessed Sacrament. Your little prayer hour will give you the strength to get through each day. You can pray for your own soul to reduce your purgatory, or for other souls that are in great need. Keep faithful to your daily regimen of prayer, and you will find yourself stronger in facing temptations."*

I could see some people adoring and worshiping Jesus in His Blessed Sacrament at Adoration. Jesus said: *"My people, I have always encouraged you to make special visits to My Blessed Sacrament so you could share your troubles and your love for Me. Some people have suggested to have some quiet time without prayers so you can truly behold and enjoy being in My Presence. Being before Me helps you to slow down and appreciate My gift to you that you can be before your God and adore and love Me. I give special blessings of grace to all who visit Me. I am an oasis of grace and peace in an evil world of sin and chaos. When you are in the worldly environment, it is hard to focus on prayer, so come and visit Me because you cannot find My peace in worldly things."*

Friday, March 17, 2006:

At the MOM Conference, Woodland Hills, California I could see a valley of beautiful green trees and it was very lush with green grass. Jesus said: *"My people, I am showing you a land of milk and honey as I promised My people while they were still in the desert. I fed them the manna that sustained them for food. This is a preview of the peace and joy that I bring all of My faithful when I sustain you with the Bread of Life in My Consecrated Host. When you feed on My Real Presence in My Eucharist, your soul is intimately united with Me, God the Father, and God the Holy Spirit. I ask only that you receive Me worthily with a clean soul free of any mortal sin so you do not commit a sin of sacrilege against My Blessed Sacrament. You have Confession available to you to cleanse your souls so you are always worthy to receive Me. Holy Communion is a union of our two hearts in a perfect love with your Lord.*

Give thanks to Me for My gift of Myself to you that even the angels do not receive. You are given the grace in My Blessed Sacrament to heal all of your past sins and this builds up your spiritual strength to avoid sin in the future. Give glory and praise to your God who has paid the ransom for your sins and blesses you with My peace and love."

Saturday, March 18, 2006:

At MOM Conference, Woodland Hills, California I could see a large ship flying a flag of the United States. It moved out of port and sailed into the sunset. Jesus said: *"My people, just as you have personal sin, there is also a collective national sin which each nation chooses by its own actions. You have read the history of My people in Scripture on how they abandoned their Lord and worshiped the idols of foreign gods. Even with Abraham and Moses giving them instruction, they reverted back to their old sinful ways. Their punishment was destruction and the Babylonian Exile where they were defeated in battle. This image of an American ship sailing off into the sunset, is a preview of your own Babylonian Exile. You also are giving in to sinful ways of adultery, fornication, and homosexual acts. You have made lust and avarice your new idols before Me. You also are killing many in unprovoked wars and abortions. How can I bless a nation that has taken prayer out of your schools, My Ten Commandments out of your courts, and are now accepting New Age teachings and the occult? You also, America, will face defeat from your neighbors by the undermining of your finances and military by the one world people. They are destroying the roots of your government and weakening you for the attacks on your country both from without and within by natural disasters. Much of your destruction and disease will be man-made and you will be in exile at My refuges. Have patience and trust in Me for I will vanquish all of these evil ones, and I will renew the face of the earth with a new heavens and a new earth in preparation for My Era of Peace. Just as I vindicated My people in Israel, I will also vindicate My faithful remnant. Then you will revel in My victory, and My peace will again reign."*

Later, at MOM Conference, Woodland Hills, California I could see the tops of many houses near the ocean and the Lord was pointing to all of the households in need of prayer. Jesus said: *"My people, many times I have asked you to pray for the poor souls in purgatory, and especially for those whom no one is praying for. In today's message I not only want you also to pray for poor sinners, but also pray for those souls whom no one is praying for. These souls on earth have not yet been judged and these eternal lives have not been determined as with God or against God. Pray the most for souls that are on the path to hell and need a miracle of grace to be converted. You have time to be saved up until your dying breath, but if there is no advocate of prayer for these sinners, their souls could be lost. Pray fervently and persistently especially for your family members. Your prayers, deeds, and good example could be the means of saving souls in your family. Family prayer is powerful for the souls of your family members. Let your children or grandchildren see that you are praying your rosaries or your Liturgy of the Hours. If they are open to your suggestion, let them pray with you. Your most important mission on earth is to save as many souls from hell as you can. You cannot force souls to love Me, but you can pray that they are disposed to being converted. Pray for My angels to guard your children from the evil ones and the evil distractions of the world. Give glory and praise to Me when one soul turns from their sinful ways to love Me. I am the father of all of My prodigal children, and all of heaven rejoices also when one soul is converted. Continue in your prayers for souls because these souls will be eternally grateful that you cared enough to try and help bring them to Me to be saved."*

Sunday, March 19, 2006:

At MOM Conference, Woodland Hills, California I could see myself on some high mountains and the lower hills appeared to be made out of silver and were attractive to man. Jesus said: *"My people, this view of the high mountains represents the spiritual high that your people are on at this retreat. It is good to be with Me in the love of your faithful as you are being nourished in the knowledge of your faith. This experience can be shared with your friends when you return home. You are also here on a moral high ground so you can be strengthened to speak out of My Word on the moral issues of your day. You must be willing to defend your faith even against the immorality that you see among your own family and friends. Do not deny Me by your silence, but be ready to witness how people should live responsibly in following My laws. Show love to all of those people that you meet and you will be imitating My unconditional love. This silver look to the lowlands represents the glitter and attraction of worldly things and money. My faithful need to survive, but you must be good examples to others so that you witness to a simple life without extravagant spending. Remember to always be sharing what you have with the poor and the needy of your family and the world. Most of all witness your love for Me in your visits to My tabernacle, your Masses, and your prayer life. Be attentive also to all of the spiritual poor who need your prayers and conversion from their sinful lifestyles. Even if you are in the minority in this evil age, strive to perfect your souls and the souls around you. Do not be angry if you must suffer difficulties because all of you are tested by the rigors of life. Come to Me in your daily prayer so you can always be renewed and never grow tired of loving Me and loving your neighbor."*

Later, at MOM Conference Woodland Hills, California I could see many people in a line bringing their cloaks to be washed by Jesus and many were kneeling before the altar. Later, I saw Jesus washing the feet of these people. Jesus said: *"My people, your theme for this conference has been to be reconciled. This vision is all about confessing your sins and allowing Me to wash your garments so you will be worthy to receive Me in Holy Communion, and to come to My Great Banquet in heaven. The other symbolic actions are when I washed the feet of those whose cloaks were cleansed. This symbol of cleansing the dirt from their feet is a representation of My Redemption of all souls by cleansing them with My redeeming Blood. The Blood of the Lamb is the Divine sacrifice of Mine that will make all of My faithful worthy of entering heaven before My heavenly Father. If you are to enter heaven, you must be cleansed of your sins in Confession and be reconciled with Me and your neighbor. You must be willing to forgive others even as I forgive you in My prayer of the 'Our Father'. You say this prayer often, but can you truly seek others' forgiveness of your sins as well as forgiving others their sins against you. When you truly love one another, you will have a forgiving heart even as I forgive everyone unconditionally."*

Monday, March 20, 2006:

At Thermal, California in front of the Luminous Cross I could see a simple picture next to the Luminous Cross. Jesus said: *"My people, as you look at this simple picture, this should help you to understand the simple life and faith that is found in this dwelling. All of My faithful should also try to live simply with a simple faith as that of a child. Let the graces of this miracle touch your heart and may My love also settle in your souls. I call on all of you to return your love to Me and to share My love with all of those around you. This Luminous Cross represents My love in how I died for all of humanity. I am your Redeemer and it is My Blood that is shed for all of you so your sins are cleansed from your souls. Look on this Luminous Cross and give praise and thanks to Me for all that I have given you. As you receive Me in Holy Com-*

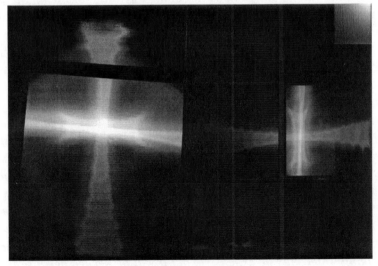

Luminous Cross

munion, you are experiencing My intimate love in My Real Presence. Be thankful to this family for allowing you to share the miracle on this door. Pray for this family as they are so generous to you in allowing you into their home."

Wednesday, March 22, 2006:

At Holy Name after Communion I could see someone taking a picture from a narrow viewpoint and then the view expanded into a broad landscape. Jesus said: *"My people, this vision is contrasting the difference between a narrow viewpoint and a broad viewpoint or the bigger picture. At times you are so focused on your own life with all of your cares and schedules that you miss or ignore everything else that is going on around you. Only by listening to and watching others' needs can you see other opportunities of grace in helping others. I have given each person enough grace to endure their own hardships, but I always leave the door open for you to help each other as well. In addition to physical needs, you can also see this same viewpoint concerning spiritual needs. You take care of your own prayer life, but you can see the spiritual needs of others as the young girl that had drug addictions and demon influences. It is important to take advantage of these physical and spiritual needs of others in how you can help someone instead of committing sins of omission by not doing anything for them. So look beyond your own life's experiences so you are aware of the physical and spiritual needs of others."*

Later, at St. Theodore's Adoration I could see a net over the water about to be lowered to catch some fish. Jesus said: *"My people, many countries rely on ocean fish for their food and their livelihoods. Unfortunately, so many ships are taking too many fish and they are not giving the fish a long enough time to be replenished. Because of the changing fish patterns, more fish are being grown in fish farms which are not as nutritious because of what they feed the fish. Many signs in the North and in the ocean currents are showing the effects of global warming. Record warm temperatures are being recorded in winter areas all over the world. The various wildlife are showing the effects of man's pollution in many areas. Droughts and fresh water needs are major concerns in poor countries. Conversion of salty seawater to drinking water may be expensive, but it will be needed because fresh water sources are getting harder to find. Pray that thirsty, starving people may be helped in getting enough fresh water to drink so there will be less deaths from bad water. Man needs to see the link between his abuses of nature and all the weather changes and pollution which are affecting your water and fishing catches."*

Thursday, March 23, 2006:

At St. John the Evangelist after Communion I could see a circling cloud like a hurricane get stronger and more violent. Jesus said: *"My people, this vision of a powerful hurricane, as the recent 180 mph cyclone in Australia, is how your storms will become stronger as the current warming trend warms the oceans. With warmer waters to feed the hurricanes, you could see more Category 5 storms than you have seen in the past. More violent storms could cause higher damage wherever they come ashore. With such threats to Southern coastlines increasing, more people will be moving inland as insurance companies will avoid insuring these areas. Even much of the damage from last year's storms has yet to be replaced because of the reluctance of insurance companies and the government to pay out huge sums for repairs. Any future damage will face the same problems, so the financial risk of living on the seashore will be too heavy for most people. Some of this damage has natural causes, some has been punishment for sin, and some has been accentuated by your microwave weather making machines. These strong storms, as in Australia, will become more the norm wherever cyclones or hurricanes occur. Pray for the people in these areas that they can evacuate early enough to minimize any loss of life, but more damage can be expected."*

At the prayer group at our house I could see a cat and a vision of a younger Cecilia. Jesus said: *"My people, Cecilia wants Me to convey to you some of her words of concern for her family members. She prays that there will be peace between her siblings over any inheritance. She knows how delicate her daughter's finances are and they are not the best, but Cecilia's heart goes out to both her daughter and her son. She asked for prayers for this situation. She is a loving person and wants peace among those whom she has left behind."*

I could see an old comfortable chair that was slowly disintegrating away. Jesus said: *"My people, many of you are comfortable in the way that you are living in America today. This chair falling apart means that you are going to suffer much as the days of tribulation come upon your* people. *Many of your comforts will be taken away as the microchips will be forced on you in smart cards first and then mandatory chips in the body. Refuse to take these chips in the body. When you do not take chips in your body, you will lose your money and your ability to buy and sell. I will call you to My refuges with your guardian angels for protection and to provide for your needs. You will suffer a purgatory on earth, but your faith will save your souls."*

I could see the suffering Jesus when He was scourged, when He carried His cross, and when He died by crucifixion. Jesus said: *"My people, each Lent you walk with Me through My Passion and death where I suffered dearly that all of you could be redeemed with My Most Precious Blood. Whatever difficulty or suffering that you are going through should be offered up to Me in My suffering, and I will help you to bear all of your life's burdens. As you suffer more in the end times, call on My graces to help you to endure this tribulation. Those, who remain faithful to the end through all persecution, will enjoy My Era of Peace and the joy of being with Me in the glory of heaven."*

I could see some passengers on an airplane and they had to suffer through turbulent winds and the uncertainty if their lives would be spared. Jesus said: *"My people, as you travel through life, you are like these people wondering how you will survive. It is your trust in Me by faith that will bring you through all of life's trials. The captured woman for ten years claimed it was her prayers on her rosary and trust in Me that got her through her long captivity. You know I am always at your side to call on My Name to help you in the worst of circumstances. All things are possible with Me and My angels are guarding you from evil at all times."*

I could see one lamp held high that dispelled the darkness in a large room. Jesus said: *"My people, My apostle John wrote of Me as a Light in the darkness throughout all of his writings. This Light is like an eternal flame that will never go out because it is a symbol of My victory over sin and evil in the world. Before I came on the earth, no one could come to heaven and all the faithful souls to God had to go to a place for the dead that was devoid of My Presence. Once I came to the earth and redeemed all of mankind, now those, who were purified, could come to heaven and enjoy eternal peace with Me in My beatific vision. This is a blessing beyond compare that has given hope to everyone that is faithful to God. But woe to those, who do not accept Me and do not seek My forgiveness, for they will truly suffer in hell eternally without experiencing My Presence."*

I could see a huge rainbow in a light rain with sunlight passing through the mist. Jesus said: *"My people, you are a rainbow people that have a promise of eternal life if you consecrate yourselves to My love. The rainbow was a covenant that I made with humanity that*

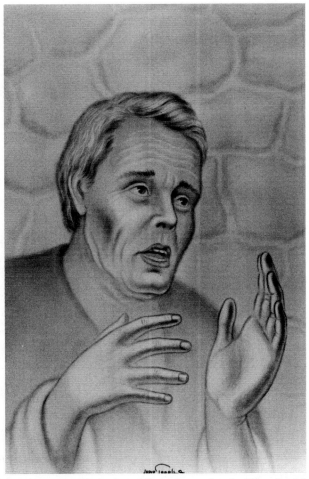

I would not ever flood the world again with water as in the Flood with Noah. But I mentioned in Scripture how you will know of the end times coming when it will be an evil time as in the days of Noah. I have made a new covenant with My people that My grace will be a saving rainbow that will protect you from all of the evil one's temptations and any attempts to steal your souls from Me."

I could see someone kneeling and praying their rosary and the Blessed Virgin Mary was holding up a rosary to act as her mantle of protection over her children. Mary said: *"My dear children, I want to thank all of you for praying My rosary and I am entrusting your petitions with My Son, (Jesus). The rosary is a powerful weapon against all the evil in your world, and you can have My Son present among you where two or more are gathered in prayer. Do not be worried or anxious as the persecution of Christians will become more apparent. Do not take up arms to fight these evil ones, but pick up your rosaries in prayer, and all of heaven will do battle for you in this world. My Son and I love you all so dearly,*

and we will not lose one of you who are faithful to us in love and prayer."

Friday, March 24, 2006:

At St. John the Evangelist after Communion I could see a tree with many branches spread out. Jesus said: *"My people, you are a worm of a man and so much a part of My creation. As you look around at all of the plants and animals, they have a plan and instincts of how to live. All of humanity is directed by Me as well, except that you have been given free will with the ability to love or not. You also have a soul and a spiritual body that lives forever and is inside your physical body which is mortal. The tree with the branches in the vision represents My people who are a part of Me as in My Mystical Body. You are the branches and I am the vine. I have given each of you a plan for your life with all of your unique talents to fulfill your mission. It is up to each one of you to discern this mission and follow My Divine Will. When you consecrate everything over to Me, you are in harmony with Me as all the rest of My creation acts accordingly. When man follows his own will in sin and abuses nature as I created it, then you have chaos in nature, wars, killing, and nature is manipulated and rebelling against you. Pray and keep your focus on Me every day, and you can do your part to bring peace to this world that you live in and are a part of."*

Later, at St. Theodore's tabernacle I could see a satellite sending out pulse waves toward the earth and they were not communications but a new weapon. Jesus said: *"My people, your scientists have already used laser guns and nuclear bombs to destroy things. Now, they have developed an EMP pulse weapon that can destroy chips and cause power outages. The vision shows how these new weapons could be placed in satellites with large arrays of solar panels to power this gun. When this technology is used from space, the user could attack cities at will to paralyze all electrical devices that use microchips. Many of these weapons and nuclear bombs in the wrong hands could destroy America's economy overnight. Pray that these weapons are not used, or many lives could be lost. This kind of terrorist attack could be far more deadly and longer lasting than the previous airplane attacks."*

Saturday, March 25: (Annunciation)

At St. Ann's Church after Communion I could see a vision of Our Blessed Mother brought down from heaven as a chosen mother since creation. Jesus said: *"My people, throughout many verses of the Old Testament, Salvation History would come through the Jewish people and a Messiah was promised to save the people from their sins. Many prophets foretold My coming to earth, but the Jewish people thought that I would come as a king or a ruler to conquer the Romans, and not as a poor carpenter. For this reason My own people had difficulty in accepting My proclamation as the Son of God, and they crucified Me as a blasphemer. In Isaiah's words:* (Isaiah 7:14) 'Therefore the Lord himself will give you this sign; the Virgin shall be with child, and bear a son, and shall name Him Emmanuel.' *My Blessed Mother had to be sinless without a man's influence and a virgin from this prophecy. I could not have an earthly father by a sexual union because I have only one Father in heaven. So My Blessed Mother conceived Me after her 'fiat' to St.*

Gabriel through the power of the Holy Spirit. The paternity of My birth was a stumbling block for St. Joseph, but the angel explained to him about the Virgin Birth from the Holy Spirit. Then he took his betrothed into his home. The origin of My birth was a stumbling block also for the Jewish people who still were in disbelief of Me as a God-man. My Incarnation as a man was a gift of Myself to share in your sufferings. Rejoice on this feast day of the announcement of My conception in My Blessed Mother's womb. This is the beginning of My presence on earth, and a fulfillment of the coming of the Messiah."

Sunday, March 26, 2006:

At Holy Name after Communion I could see a small white cross and then it grew into a large brown cross. Jesus said: *"My people, during Lent you pray the Stations of the Cross and you meditate on how I suffered for your sins. This represents the small white cross in the vision. Then there are your own personal struggles in life that you face every day. This large brown cross is what you suffer to survive in this life. Working hard for your salary, paying your bills, and taking care of your family can be trying at times, but you can always call on My help and grace to relax and comfort your stress. You should have trust and hope that I will support you through the worst of circumstances. I have helped you in the past, and I will help you now. Give praise and thanks to Me because you will never be tested beyond your means. Sometimes you may be humbled to ask others to help you, and you should be generous in helping others in great need."*

Later, at St. Theodore's tabernacle I could see a street that seemed to be in Washington, D.C. and people were running down the street completely terrified. Jesus said: *"My people, this vision is very serious of a coming event in Washington, D.C. As time draws closer, I will be giving you more details. Pray for the people of your country for you are about to witness terrorist events and natural disasters that will be bringing you to your knees. Many messages and warnings have been given to America to improve your sinful lives, but people are not listening or repenting. Your people are growing worse in homosexual marriages and using internet pornography. All of the destruction, that is occurring, is being brought on America as a consequence of your own sins. Pray much for your families that are falling apart in divorce and promiscuous activity outside of marriage. Your sinful activity is as evil as Sodom and Gomorrah and the people of Noah's day. See that many of the signs of the days of tribulation are all around you."*

Monday, March 27, 2006:

At St. John the Evangelist after Communion I could see a spiral staircase going up many flights of stairs. Jesus said: *"My people, during Lent you are trying to do extra things to improve your spiritual life, but in this age of evil you are being called to strive for this same holiness throughout the whole year. Many of you do not realize the battle against evil spirits going on all around you. With all of the evil influences on your TV, in your movies, and in people's evil actions, there are more people walking around under the influence of evil spirits. You need to have blessed sacramentals on your person at all times to protect yourselves from demon attacks. Where possible even have your homes blessed to keep evil spirits from entering. I have asked you to pick up your daily crosses on your way to Calvary with Me. Going up the hill of Calvary is represented in the vision of a spiral staircase. It means not just to struggle through life, but also you must be looking constantly for ways to improve your spiritual life. You are striving for perfection and the demons try to retard your growth, so moving forward in your perfection is an uphill battle."*

Later, at St. Theodore's tabernacle I could see a shovel and a flashing mirror. Jesus said: *"My people, Lent is a time to reflect on your actions and motives to see if they are following My plan for your life. At times you spend too much time watching TV to be entertained instead of doing things to save souls. Other times you are curious to watch the world news to see what is happening, when you could be praying more. When you examine your actions for the day, you can see which things are useful for coming to heaven and which things are selfish and leading you away from Me. You all could profit by analyzing your behavior so you could learn from your mistakes and improve your holiness. With earthly distractions always around you, it is hard to keep your focus on serving Me. This is why you should be calling on Me in constant prayer to show you the best way to imitate My love. Keep your souls cleansed of sin in frequent Confession, and you will have My grace so you can carry out My mission to help save souls."*

Tuesday, March 28, 2006:

At Holy Name after Communion I could see a little hill with an entrance to the top and a cross waiting for someone. On the top of the hill there was a small forest of trees and bright sunlight. Jesus said: *"My people, this hill represents the coming tribulation time when some of My faithful will be martyred, and the rest will be seeking My protection at the refuges. The waiting cross is for those who will be suffering for Me instead of giving up their faith. All of those, who will suffer martyrdom, will become instant saints. The rest of My faithful will suffer losing all of their comforts and possessions when they come to My refuges. It is difficult to give everything over to Me in total consecration, because many are like the rich man in the Gospel who did not want to give up his riches and walked away from Me. The evil ones will try to force chips in the body for control, but you must refuse them, even if you may be faced with death or prison for My Name's sake. They will also try to force you to worship the Antichrist, but you must only worship Me. This truly will be a choice for Me, or for the Antichrist. Those, who choose to follow Me, will give up everything and be rewarded in heaven. Those, who choose the Antichrist, will have temporary comfort on earth, but an eternal discomfort in hell later. Choose peace and love with Me, instead of war and hate from the evil one."*

Later, at St. Theodore's Adoration I could see the back end of an old car being used for a garden. Jesus said: *"My people, you are having a serious problem with illegal immigrants crossing the border to try and get a low paying job. There are many low paying physical jobs that few people are willing to take because it is hard to make a living on such a job. Employers, who have difficulty getting such workers, are willing to hire illegal immigrants for low wages. As long as such employers give them jobs, there will be an incentive for poor people to risk crossing the border for having a better life than in Mexico. Your government is having a hard time to determine how to handle so many millions of people in a humane way, but also how to keep terrorists from entering as well. Pray for your leaders to choose an equitable law that would be fair to all parties. Many hospitals and social services are being overburdened in your Southern states. It is long coming that such a problem is finally being faced. Many controls by IDs and smart cards will be used in the name of security to handle these problems. See the control of your people will be coming to control illegal immigrants, but it will put stress on your legal citizens and legal immigrants as well."*

Wednesday, March 29, 2006:

At St. John the Evangelist after Communion I could see a large garbage compacter packing up the trash. Jesus said: *"My people, now that the temperatures are warming, many are cleaning up their yards from all of the winter debris and wind storms. Lent comes in the spring time and it is like a spiritual spring cleaning of your souls. You desire a good appearance for your yard and your person, but you should also desire a good appearance for your soul. This means regular or frequent Confession can root out your old habitual sins and offer your sins up to Me. Do not let your sins hold you captive, but you must let go of your earthly desires to be spiritually free. If necessary, ask your confessor for some suggestions of how best to avoid habitual sin. If you do not have a desire to shed them on your way to more perfection, you will be holding back your spiritual improvement. The more you conquer your sins with My help, the more you will feel the joy of your freedom to follow Me closely. All the angels and saints are singing for joy because the saints have lifted off their sinful baggage, and they are free to do God's bidding. Let this Lent be profitable for your souls as you make every attempt to come closer to Me without any clinging to earthly desires. The more you can cleanse these bad sins now, the less you will have to purify in purgatory."*

Later, at St. Theodore's Adoration I could see parts of a bridge washed out by a rain swollen river. Jesus said: *"My people, this vision shows the result of heavy rains that could cause rain swollen rivers to overflow their banks and wash out bridges. In the spring months your weather will continue to test you with tornadoes and downpours of rain. Some areas could suffer power outages and lost houses to flooding. People continue to build houses on flood plains or next to rivers that have flooded in the past. Pray that people will get sufficient warning to evacuate any flooded areas. Much of your hurricane ravaged cities are still vulnerable to any future storms. Those, who live by rivers and oceans, will be more susceptible to more storm damage. America will continue to suffer from these natural disasters as your oceans continue to heat up. More planning by your governments is needed to provide for the people who lose their homes and jobs in these disasters."*

Thursday, March 30, 2006:

At St. John the Evangelist after Communion I could see a fisherman fishing and the fish on the line took the line all the way to the end of the reel. Jesus said: *"My people, sometimes man does not fully comprehend My infinite love and My unending forgiveness. A person may have committed many sins while they were away from Confession for many years. They may feel that they are too unworthy for Me to forgive them. Some people, as in this vision of being at the end of a fishing line, feel that they have no place to go and that God has abandoned them. I tell you, do not be discouraged or in despair, but come to your Lord and I will forgive you of your sins. I always love everyone and it is you who limit your love for Me. I am also willing to forgive every repentant sinner of their sins. I am the Good Shepherd always searching for My lost sheep and souls. There are many desperate souls that are searching for Me in all of the wrong earthly traps. When you pray for My help, I will listen to your prayer, but you must make some intentions to reach out to My love by opening the door to your heart. Without denying yourself of earthly desires and seeking My forgiveness, it will be hard to change your life to My ways. Think love of Me and your neighbor and this love will set you free of all of your sins and earthly distractions. Worship Me only and your soul will be saved by My grace."*

Later, at the prayer group at Holy Name Adoration I could see where the twin towers had fallen and how America was humbled by this destruction. Jesus said: *"My people, many hurts of those who died in 2001 are still with your people. The twin towers destruction was a wake up call for America as to how far terrorism could be felt. There is much controversy about who helped these terrorists, but it definitely affected America's economy, even as Katrina has had a lasting effect. These events are not over and you could see more terrorist attacks to come. Pray for America as you will be tested enough to bring you to your knees by disasters."*

I could see some scaffolds being made for some public executions. In the past we have seen gallows for hanging, but in the end times the evil ones will kill people by Guillotines. Jesus said: *"My people, you are seeing Christians persecuted and killed in many Moslem countries. I have shown you the Antichrist as a Moslem person, and there will be some of My faithful martyred for their faith. I have taught My followers not to kill in wars but to pray for your persecutors. Even though the Moslems will kill some of you, I will protect the rest in My refuges. Be assured that this evil reign will be brief and then I will come victorious against all of the evil ones as they will be chained in hell. My Era of Peace will be your reward."*

I could see buildings falling from an earthquake in the West and fires were starting from the broken gas lines. Jesus said: *"My people, I have given you several visions and messages about coming earthquakes in California, especially around San Francisco. These fault lines have been active and any day you could see a major quake in a populated area. Pray for these people who are living sinful lives in defiance of My Commandments."*

I could see earthquakes in the middle of America and continued problems from tornadoes and hurricanes. Jesus said: *"My people, in the West your people build your buildings stronger to endure earthquakes. In the middle of your country your buildings could face more destruction because they have not seen serious damage for over one hundred years. Your storms also have taken their toll on your homes and workplaces. Be prepared for more disasters this year as they will continue to test your comforts."*

I could see some flames scorching many acres of our extremely dry areas in California, Texas, and more recently in Florida. Jesus said: *"My people, fire has ravaged your land even during the winter months. Normally your dry spells have occurred in the summer months when your weather is hot and dry. Now, you are seeing fires occur in both seasons and they will continue to worsen as your temperatures all over are increasing. Pray for those people who are suffering losses as a result of these fires."*

I could see an area of a school with pots, pans, and ladles hanging where chefs were learning how to cook. Jesus said: *"My people, in hotels and on cruise ships you see some rich cuisine, but much food is being wasted. Yet in other parts of the world the poor would love to live off of the scraps of these tables. Remember how I talked about the rich man and Lazarus, the beggar. The rich man ignored Lazarus, even though he could have fed him. After the judgment the rich man found the flames of hell, while Lazarus was rewarded in heaven. America is like the rich man and the poor of the world are like Lazarus. Do not forget the poor because you are feeding Me in them when you give donations to the poor."*

I could see some horses that people used to use for transportation before we had cars. Jesus said: *"My people, for years man used beasts of burden as horses, mules, and oxen for carrying things and plowing fields. Today, man is in love with his cars, trucks, and SUVs. To run these vehicles you are consuming many millions of gallons of fuel from oil and other sources. You have seen much pollution from running these vehicles and your power plants that run all of your favorite electrical devices. See how you are affecting your environment with all of your modern inventions. Your consumption of fuels has to change because this pollution could change the weather patterns of the world. A simpler life would give you less stress and fewer problems associated with your earthly comforts and pleasures."*

Friday, March 31, 2006:

At Holy Trinity Church, Louisville, Kentucky I could see some water and a large brick bridge going over it. At first the bridge was breaking apart at the middle, but then Jesus put it back together with His love. Jesus said: *"My people, every time that you receive Me in Holy Communion or visit Me in My tabernacle, you are intimately receiving My love which binds your soul to Me. Even though you break your relationship with Me in sin, as this bridge falling apart, I heal your sins in Confession, and My love restores this love relationship to its full glory. Divine Love is all powerful and I rain down My love on all of you, even as you see My physical rain enrich the soil for your crops. My spiritual rain of love falls on each soul and it nourishes your love for Me. Be grateful and give thanks to Me that I have given Myself to you in My consecrated Host. The God of All Nations is always present to each of you. All you need to do is reach out to Me and accept the mission that I gave you. I inspire all of you to love Me and your neighbor as yourself. The joy and peace in your heart is how I share My love with you, and you in turn share your love with Me. You see how I build bridges of love to everyone, and I want My followers to go out into the world and build bridges of love with each other also."*

Index

Prepare for the Great Tribulation and the Era of Peace

Jesus spiritual garbage man (Jesus) — 2/20/2006
Jesus as King not accepted as Messiah (Jesus) — 1/23/2006
joy, love of God signs of saint (Jesus) — 2/21/2006
judgment hungry, sick, dying (Jesus) — 3/16/2006
justice only on Jesus' return (Jesus) — 2/28/2006
killing lives is not an option (Jesus) — 2/3/2006
leaders servants to all (Jesus) — 3/15/2006
Lent improves spiritual life (Jesus) — 3/16/2006
Lent self-denial for penance (Jesus) — 1/26/2006
Lenten devotions make holier people (Jesus) — 3/5/2006
Lenten regimen good for the soul (Jesus) — 3/9/2006
leprosy, spiritual change from unclean (Jesus) — 2/12/2006
life needs protection (Jesus) — 2/3/2006
life review judgment shown in Warning (Jesus) — 1/9/2006
light beam for moving objects (Jesus) — 2/19/2006
Light of God seen at Warning, death (Jesus) — 1/8/2006
living Scriptures in actions is important (Jesus) — 2/25/2006
Living Water of God grace, peace & rest (Jesus) — 2/23/2006
loaves & fish multiplied, 7 & 12 used (Jesus) — 2/7/2006
love everyone everyday of the year (Jesus) — 2/9/2006
love for God agape love (Jesus) — 2/14/2006
love of God greatest desire of soul (Jesus) — 2/22/2006
Luminous Cross give thanks and praise (Jesus) — 3/20/2006
Lyon, John Paul death of young child (Jesus) — 2/4/2006
magnetic pole shifts spread Northern Lights (Jesus) — 1/12/2006
man's abuses nature rebels (Jesus) — 3/24/2006
man's call listen for God's voice (Jesus) — 1/15/2006
manufacturing job losses could cause riots (Jesus) — 2/2/2006
manufacturing jobs being destroyed by US policies (Jesus) — 1/24/2006
marriage place of Jesus' 1st miracle (Jesus) — 1/7/2006
marriage & divorce life commitment needed (Jesus) — 2/24/2006
marry in Church than live in fornication (Jesus) — 2/24/2006
martyrs and refuges for others (Jesus) — 1/2/2006
martyrs may have to die for faith (Jesus) — 1/13/2006
Mary's encouragement take rosaries,not arms (Mary) — 3/23/2006
Mass prayer of thanksgiving (Jesus) — 3/7/2006
Mauer, Dick funeral Mass (Jesus) — 1/5/2006
mercy of God in 2nd chance to change (Jesus) — 2/20/2006
microwave pulses trigger epidemic diseases (Jesus) — 3/1/2006
Middle East war threatens more countries (Jesus) — 1/19/2006
mine violations to be investigated (Jesus) — 1/4/2006
miners' deaths not revealed properly (Jesus) — 1/4/2006
miners killed West Virginia tragedy (Jesus) — 1/4/2006
mines, mudslides need safety improvements (Jesus) — 2/23/2006
mission everyone called by God (Jesus) — 1/22/2006
mission in life given to each person (Jesus) — 1/13/2006
mission, important save souls from hell (Jesus) — 3/18/2006
monastic prayer life keeps focus on Jesus (Jesus) — 2/10/2006
monastic retreats removes distractions (Jesus) — 3/16/2006
money desires are distraction from God (Jesus) — 2/27/2006
money, possessions do not make gods (Jesus) — 1/27/2006
morality in America also declining (Jesus) — 2/17/2006

Moslems killing Christians (Jesus) — 3/30/2006
movies, TV, friends bad influence on children (Jesus) — 3/12/2006
natural gas lower cost when warmer (Jesus) — 1/26/2006
nature despoiled by man's manipulation (Jesus) — 2/16/2006
nature manipulated man will pay (Jesus) — 2/13/2006
nature, population confirming evil of abortion (Jesus) — 1/23/2006
needs of others opportunities for graces (Jesus) — 3/22/2006
New Age teachings to come into churches (Jesus) — 2/12/2006
New Orleans needs to repent of sins (Jesus) — 3/2/2006
New Orleans still cleaning up (Jesus) — 1/18/2006
North Korea & Iran threats to world peace (Jesus) — 1/17/2006
nuclear war too dangerous (Jesus) — 3/9/2006
omission, sins of time & money for poor (Jesus) — 3/16/2006
one world people are running America (Jesus) — 2/17/2006
one world people behind demise of America (Jesus) — 1/20/2006
one world people challenged on ports (Jesus) — 3/9/2006
one world people destroying finances, military (Jesus) — 3/18/2006
one world people profit from wars (Jesus) — 3/9/2006
one world people trying to destroy middle class (Jesus) — 1/24/2006
one world people want chips in everyone (Jesus) — 1/7/2006
open hearts to God require letting go (Jesus) — 3/13/2006
pagan practices human sacrifices, idol worship (Jesus) — 1/30/2006
passports to require smart cards (Jesus) — 1/6/2006
peace & love better than wars & hate (Jesus) — 1/9/2006
peace and love start in the home (Jesus) — 2/23/2006
peacemakers call to heal divisions (Jesus) — 1/9/2006
peacemakers, be than war makers (Jesus) — 3/2/2006
persecution of Christians will become threatening again (Jesus) — 1/26/2006
pillars of Church models of faith to others (Jesus) — 3/3/2006
pollution, fuel affecting environment (Jesus) — 3/30/2006
poor sinners pray for lost souls (Jesus) — 3/18/2006
port selling to Arabs security questioned (Jesus) — 3/9/2006
possession can be by multiple demons (Jesus) — 1/30/2006
possessions, more harder to give up (Jesus) — 3/14/2006
power grids, fuel depots targets of terrorists (Jesus) — 1/20/2006
power of God greater than all demons (Jesus) — 1/14/2006
prayer needed to stop nuclear war (Jesus) — 2/10/2006
prayer, persistent all possible with God (Jesus) — 1/10/2006
prayer, reasons for adore,bless,petition,forgive (Jesus) — 3/7/2006
Presentation in Temple Jesus' Light in world (Jesus) — 2/2/2006
pride & selfishness hold back love (Jesus) — 2/27/2006
privacy challenged by smart cards (Jesus) — 2/3/2006
Progress of man balance of nature lost (Jesus) — 2/6/2006
public witness of God needed to be saved (Jesus) — 1/3/2006
purgatory choice suffer here than there (Jesus) — 2/12/2006
quiet time with Jesus needed (Jesus) — 1/6/2006
rainbow people those saved in God (Jesus) — 3/23/2006
Real Presence in Host gift of Jesus to us (Jesus) — 2/6/2006
record storms weather patterns changing (Jesus) — 2/16/2006
refuge maker after prayer, discernment (Jesus) — 2/16/2006
refuge time sooner than you think (Jesus) — 3/6/2006
refuges miraculous protection (Jesus) — 2/15/2006

More Messages

If you would like to take advantage of more precious words from Jesus and Mary and apply them to your lives, read the first three volumes of messages and visions given to us through John's special gift. Each book contains a full year of daily messages and visions. As Jesus and Mary said in volume IV:

Listen to My words of warning, and you will be ready to share in the beauty of the Second Coming. Jesus 7/4/96
I will work miracles of conversion on those who read these books with an open mind. Jesus 9/5/96

Prepare for the Great Tribulation and the Era of Peace